AF400875

Simply DINNERS

DELICIOUSLY EASY MEALS FOR EVERY NIGHT OF THE WEEK

MANDY MILLER SIMMONDS

Acknowledgements

I would like to dedicate this book to my two sons Toby and Charlie, but would also like to acknowledge my mum and dad. Without each and every one of them, this book would not have come to fruition. My love of food clearly stemmed from my parents. But it's because of Toby and Charlie that I started cooking meals that were not only delicious, but were simple to make. I've literally tried and tested everything on them over the years and let me tell you the feedback has been unfiltered! In recent years they offered support, encouragement and I'm both astonished and proud of their vision and ability to overcome adversity. When it comes to technology and social media it's important to listen to the kids! Thank you boys.

I set up my social media account @simplyfoodbymandy eight years ago and have built up a loyal and supportive following. I'd like to thank each and everyone of you. Without you, this book would not be here, so thank you.

I want to thank the fabulous team at Meze Publishing for listening, understanding my vision and creating the most beautiful book. It's been a pleasure working with you. Thank you to Paul Gregory for taking beautiful photos of my food, after all, what is a cookbook without amazing pictures?

To Mollie Manning for the cover pic and portraits, you never fail to make me feel so comfortable in front of the camera. You always deliver exactly what I want – thank you.

To Louise Bright, for not only being my dear friend, but helping me cook, clear up and style 80 recipes in just 10 days! You know me so well, can read my mind and I love your style.

I'd also like to mention my best friend from primary school, Helen Sowman in New Zealand, who made my recipes for her family just to see if they worked, but also for that all-important feedback. Clyde, Ella, Pippa and Max – thank you.

To Matt Tebbutt, James Tanner and Jonathan Phang, having talented chefs endorse my book means the world. I'm truly grateful.

Finally I must say thank you to my brilliant agent Jennifer Waterman, for your continued support and for keeping things running smoothly with my brand work whilst I was writing this book. You are a gem.

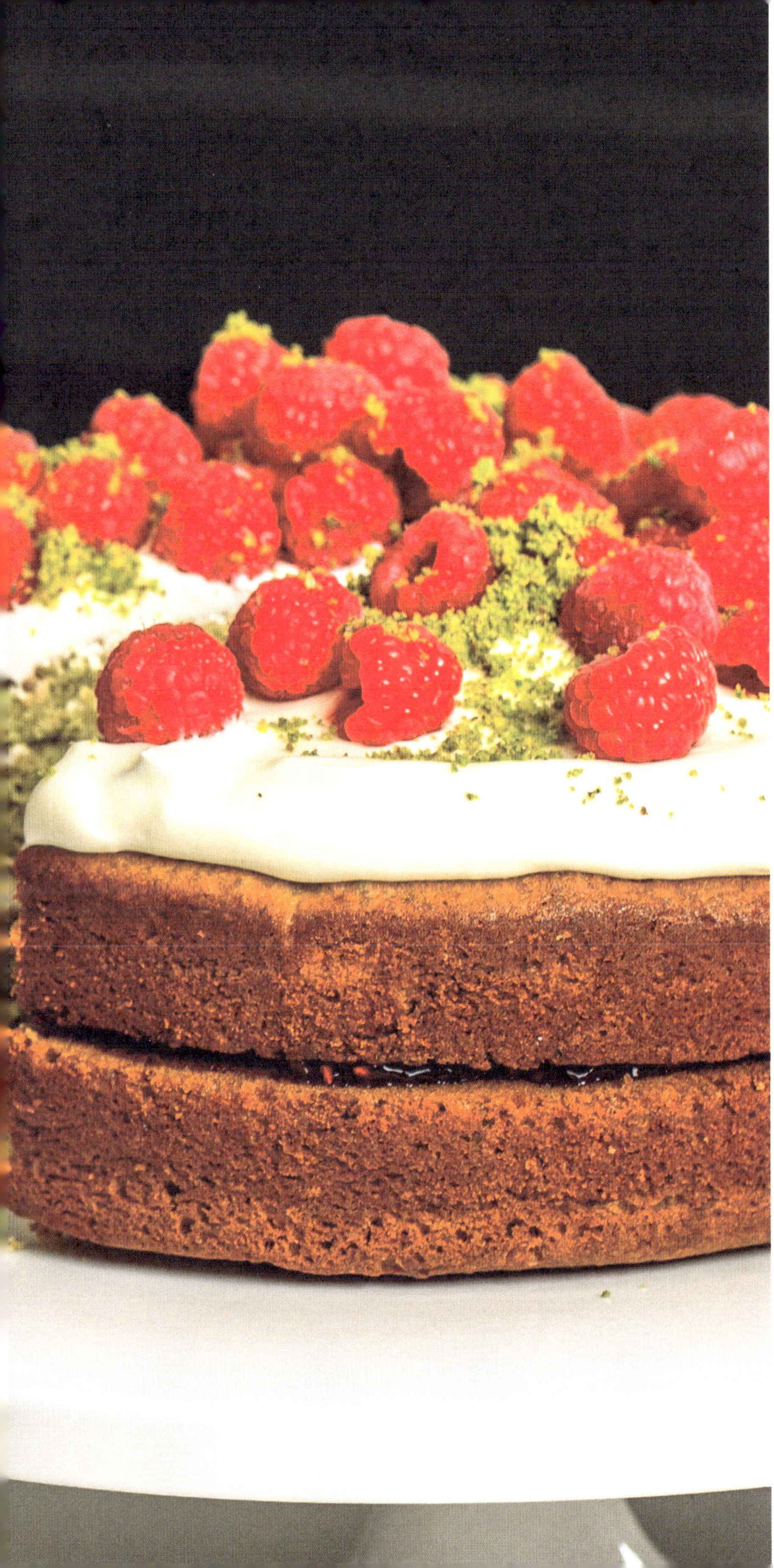

Simply DINNERS

First edition printed in 2025
ISBN: 9781915538383
Written by: Mandy Miller Simmonds
Edited by: Tay Rayner, Katie Fisher
Food photography by: Paul Gregory
(www.paulgregoryphotography.co.uk)
Portraits: Mollie Manning
(www.molliemanning.co.uk)
Designed by: Paul Cocker
Sales: Emma Toogood

Published by Meze Publishing Limited
Unit 1b, 2 Kelham Square
Kelham Riverside
Sheffield S3 8SD
Web: www.mezepublishing.co.uk
Telephone: 0114 275 7709
Email: info@mezepublishing.co.uk

My Story

Food has always been central to my life. My parents, both fantastic home cooks, set the tone for a childhood steeped in the joys of cooking and eating. Despite a modest budget, Mum approached food with creativity and confidence, never afraid to experiment. She could transform simple ingredients into adventurous meals with ease, and she showed me that cooking didn't have to be complicated to be rewarding. Dad, on the other hand, introduced me to Mediterranean flavours during family holidays to Spain and France. Those trips revolved around food, and I'll never forget the thrill of trying shellfish and grilled squid for the first time. Dad would buy mussels from the local market, and we'd clean and cook them together, making moules marinière and feeling as though we were dining like royalty.

These formative experiences sparked a lifelong passion for food. It wasn't just about sustenance; it was an adventure, a way to explore the world and bring people together.

Though food played a starring role, my first love was dancing. At 16, I joined Bird College to train full-time, dedicating my days to something I adored. While my peers lived on instant noodles, I cooked meals from scratch – simple but hearty dishes like casseroles, bolognese, and Spanish omelettes. I found joy in experimenting, stretching my budget with cheaper cuts of meat and learning how to make them shine. My friends thought I was eccentric, but they happily devoured the results.

Upon graduating, I landed a job as a dancer on cruise ships, performing in Broadway-style productions while travelling the globe. It was an exhilarating chapter of my life. From Helsinki to Hawaii, each port offered new culinary discoveries, and I seized every opportunity to explore the local food scene. My earnings often went straight to restaurants and markets, where I could immerse myself in the flavours of the region. I also befriended chefs on board, who introduced me to their national cuisines. I'll never forget the joy of tasting authentic Indian curries and breads prepared by the ship's Indian kitchen staff. Their generosity and skill deepened my appreciation for global food traditions.

But life on the seas came with its challenges. As a dancer, I was subject to weekly weigh-ins and often told to lose weight – a difficult balance when all I wanted to do was savour the incredible dishes around me. Over time, I began to miss the comforts of home, particularly the freedom to cook my own meals. After nearly a decade of dancing, I decided it was time for a change. Returning to the UK felt bittersweet, but I was ready to start the next chapter.

Shortly after coming home, I met my now ex-husband, Tris, and in 2003, we welcomed our first son, Toby, followed by Charlie in 2008. Becoming a mum was both rewarding and challenging. Many of my friends were still performing, while I found myself in a completely different world. Cooking became my anchor. It gave me a sense of purpose and allowed me to channel my creativity while caring for my family. I realised how important it was to nourish both body and mind through food, especially when balancing the demands of parenthood.

Weaning my boys brought its own joys and challenges. I loved transforming our evening meals into nutritious purées for them, experimenting with flavours to keep things interesting. Though some attempts were more successful than others, I relished the process and even developed a system for freezing portions in ice cube trays – a method that felt innovative (and economical!) at the time. Friends often asked for my recipes, and I was happy to share tips that made their lives a bit easier.

When Toby was young, we moved from London to Kent to be closer to family. While I missed the vibrancy of London's food scene, the move offered the support network I needed. It also gave me the space to dive deeper into my passion for cooking. Entertaining became a creative outlet. Whether hosting friends or celebrating special occasions, I loved planning menus and experimenting with new ideas. Before having kids, I would spend days preparing elaborate meals. But as life grew busier, I shifted my focus to fuss-free dishes that still felt special. Sharing platters, themed dinners, and hearty meals like chilli made with chunks of meat instead of mince became my go-to solutions. These dishes were simple to prepare, could be made in advance, and kept the pressure off entertaining.

At the same time, I became determined to create meals that worked for everyone in the household. I refused to cook separate dishes for fussy eaters and took pride in crafting menus that brought the family together. I knew I wasn't alone in this struggle – many of my friends felt overwhelmed trying to please everyone at the dinner table. I wanted to show that wholesome, delicious meals could be simple and accessible.

In 2017, I took a leap and started sharing my food journey on social media. At first, it was a way to connect with others and offer practical recipes that anyone could follow. I wanted people to feel inspired, not intimidated, and to see that cooking at home could be both satisfying and straightforward. The positive response was overwhelming. Families began trying my recipes and sharing their successes, which encouraged me to keep experimenting and sharing new ideas.

Social media also taught me a lot about what people wanted from their kitchen. My most popular recipes – traybakes, curries, casseroles, pasta dishes, and 15-minute meals – reflected the need for simplicity and versatility. Through trial and error, I learned how to balance ease with impact, creating dishes that looked impressive but didn't require hours in the kitchen. I wanted my platform to be a hub for real, approachable food that suited all abilities. It was important to me that people saw my recipes as achievable, without needing to have lots of skills and equipment in the kitchen.

Building a connection with my audience became my driving force. The interaction and feedback helped me refine my style and expand my repertoire. It also had an unexpected effect on my family – my boys started trying more adventurous foods, and I became bolder in the kitchen, experimenting with new flavours and combinations.

My mission was clear: to show that great food doesn't have to be complicated. Good ingredients, a little creativity, and a focus on what really matters – flavour and enjoyment – are all you need. Cooking should be a joy, not a chore, and I'm passionate about helping people discover that for themselves.

Contents

Acknowledgements   4

My Story   8

About this Book   14

Freezer Tips   18

Kitchen Tips and Tricks   22

Family Favourites

Pulled BBQ Pork   26

Sticky Mango Chutney Chicken   28

Philly Steak Sandwich   30

Cajun Prawn Tacos with Avocado and Mango Salsa   32

Miso Chicken Poke Bowls   34

Spiced Honey Glazed Chicken Skewers
with Greek Salad Salsa   36

Chicken and Mushroom Pot Pie   38

Sausage Plait   40

Three Cheese Mac and Cheese
with Breadcrumb Topping   42

Special Egg Fried Rice   44

Sausage Pasta   46

Bacon and Leek Pasta Bake   48

Prawn and Pea Orzo   50

Creamy Bacon and Mushroom Pasta   52

Speedy Dinners

Sirloin Steak with Asian-style Chimichurri   56

Chicken Koftas with Tzatziki   58

Thai Beef Noodle Salad   60

Salmon Tikka Skewers with Green Chutney   62

Asian Crab Cakes   64

Salmon and Dill Fish Cakes with Tartare Sauce   66

Red Thai Prawn Ramen   68

Fish Puttanesca   70

Pil Pil Prawns   72

Indian Spiced Salmon with Yoghurt
and Coriander Sauce   74

Parma Ham Wrapped Cod with Spinach Puy Lentils
and Vine Roasted Tomatoes   76

Miso Glazed Salmon   78

Cajun Fish with Black Bean and Avocado Salsa   80

Courgette Fritters with Herby Yoghurt   82

Harissa Cauliflower Steaks with
Zhoug, Toasted Almonds and Pomegranate Seeds   84

One Pan or Pot

Peanut and Soy Chicken — 88

Chicken Saag — 90

Roast Cod, Vegetable and Potato Traybake with Salsa Verde — 92

Mushroom and Spinach Gnocchi with Burrata — 94

Chicken and Orzo Traybake — 96

Roasted Vegetable and Halloumi Traybake — 98

Moroccan Fish Tagine — 100

Thai Chicken Traybake — 102

Oven Baked Prawn and Chorizo Paella — 104

Prawn and Okra Curry — 106

Chicken Shashlik Traybake — 108

Roast Dinners

Côte de Boeuf — 112

Asparagus with Lemon and Olive Oil — 112

Roasted New Potatoes with Garlic and Thyme — 113

Salsa Verde — 113

Korean Style Pork Tenderloin — 116

Harissa Leg of Lamb — 118

Roast Sea Bream with Lemon, Shallot and Caper Dressing — 120

Roast Chicken with Fennel, Lemon, Garlic and Tarragon Butter and Tarragon Aioli — 122

Hasselback Roast Butternut Squash — 124

Whole Roast Salmon with Ginger, Chilli and Garlic — 126

Classic Rib of Beef with Red Wine Gravy and Homemade Horseradish Sauce — 128

Tandoori Slow-cooked Shoulder of Lamb with Green Chutney — 130

Nostalgia Recipes

Aubergine Parmigiana — 134

My Mum's Chicken in the Brick — 136

Veal Milanese — 138

Mum's Christmas Eve Lamb Curry — 140

My Dad's New Zealand Mussels in the Half Shell — 142

Chicken Noodle Soup — 144

Mum's Quiche — 146

Ultimate Prawn Cocktail — 148

Pork and Chutney Sausage Rolls — 150

French Dressing — 152

Simple but Delicious Tomato Sauce — 154

Chicken Liver Pâté — 156

Tuna Dip — 158

Marie's Elderflower Loaf Cake — 160

Auntie Sasa's Chocolate Pots — 162

Cheat's Trifle — 164

Sweet Treats

Apple Tarte Tatin — 168

Raspberry and Pistachio Eton Mess — 170

Chocolate and Orange Banana Bread — 172

Strawberries and Cream Cake — 174

Carrot Cupcakes — 176

Pavlova with Chantilly Cream and Summer Fruits — 178

Lemon Possets — 180

Pistachio and Raspberry Cake — 182

Coconut, Mango and Cardamom Rice Pudding — 184

Plum, Cardamom and Vanilla Cake — 186

Chocolate Chip Cookies — 188

About this Book

I've dreamed of writing this book for years, but life has a way of throwing curveballs. When Covid hit, like so many others, my world changed. By early 2021, just as life was restarting, my husband of 16 years and I separated. It was a time of upheaval, and my focus shifted to my boys as we navigated a new chapter together. Fast forward a few years and after a divorce and a house move, I felt ready to finally make this dream a reality.

This book is a reflection of my kitchen and the meals I love to cook at home. It had to be simple, approachable, reliable and, of course, delicious. Think of it as a continuation of what I share on my social media, but with a deeper dive into the recipes that mean the most to me.

For everyday dinners, I rely on tried-and-true recipes that everyone loves and finishes with a clean plate – meals so quick to disappear that I sometimes wonder if my boys inhale them! These recipes inspired the Family Favourites chapter, packed with crowd-pleasers that my best friend Helen, all the way in New Zealand, even tested on her kids, Ella, Pippa and Max.

Like many, I'm not a fan of endless washing up. That's why the One Pan or Pot chapter is dedicated to recipes that deliver big on taste while keeping things fuss-free. Cooking everything in a single dish allows flavours to mingle beautifully, creating meals that are both satisfying and economical.

For those busy nights when time is short, Speedy Dinners is your go-to. These recipes are quick to prepare, with most on the table in under 30 minutes – perfect for juggling work, school runs, or simply fitting a good meal into a hectic schedule.

My food journey wouldn't be what it is without the influence of the people closest to me. In Nostalgia, I've included recipes that hold a special place in my heart. These dishes tell the story of where my love for food began and honour the people who helped ignite that passion.

And finally, what's a cookbook without desserts? I always flip straight to the sweet section when I pick up a new cookbook, and I hope you'll do the same. Sweet Treats is a collection of comforting old favourites and a few fresh additions – all easy to make and impossible to resist.

Freezer Tips

Can I freeze it?

As a rule of thumb, it's best to freeze food when it's as fresh as possible. Freezing slows bacteria growth, but starting with fresh produce means better-tasting, higher-quality results. When buying frozen food, aim to get it into your freezer as quickly as possible. I like to bring freezer blocks in a cool bag to the shops during warmer months to keep things chilled on the way home.

Defrosting and refreezing

For the best results, defrost food slowly overnight in the fridge. Certain foods, like soups, ragù and sauces, can be cooked directly from frozen (see below for details). Avoid refreezing food that's already thawed, unless it's been cooked first.

Cooking from frozen

Some dishes – like soups, ragù, non-creamy sauces, and casseroles – can go straight from freezer to stovetop. To do this, place the frozen food in a pan, cover with a lid to trap steam, and cook on low heat until piping hot. Avoid cooking large joints of meat or poultry directly from frozen, as they won't cook evenly.

Shortcuts

- Grate frozen cheese, ginger or chillies directly into dishes for added flavour.
- Keep a pint of milk in the freezer as a backup supply.
- Store sliced bread for toasting straight from frozen in the freezer.

Wrapping and storing

Freezer burn can ruin food quickly, so it's essential to wrap items well. Use high-quality freezer bags, squeeze out as much air as possible, and seal securely. Label everything with the date for easy tracking. Laying meals flat not only saves space but also speeds up the defrosting process.

What You Can Freeze

Fresh raw meat, raw poultry, raw fish, cooked shredded chicken, hard cheese, milk, eggs, raw vegetables, roasted veggies, mashed potato, cooked rice, cooked pasta, fresh pasta (cook straight from frozen), homemade gravy, marinades, bananas, butter, bread, cakes, biscuits, muffins, pancakes, berries, wine, seeds, nuts, flour, ginger, chilli, grapes, citrus slices, tomato purée, stock, leftover bones or chicken carcasses (for stock), vegetable peelings (for stock), herbs frozen in olive oil (in ice cube trays), spices.

What You Can't Freeze

Soft cheese, yoghurt, cream, ricotta, leafy salads, dishes with crumb toppings, or pre-frozen raw meats (unless cooked).

Kitchen Tips and Tricks

Use a spoon to easily scrape the skin off ginger.

Freeze leftover herbs with olive oil in ice cube trays for quick, fresh flavour boosts.

Revive day-old bread by sprinkling it with water and baking for 4 minutes to make it fresh and crispy.

Fish needs minimal cooking; once you see white, milky juices oozing out, it's overcooked.

Rub lemon on your chopping board before preparing onions to prevent teary eyes.

Dip your spoon in flavourless oil before scooping syrup or honey to stop it from sticking.

Spend time caramelising onions for sauces – the longer they cook, the sweeter they become, adding incredible depth of flavour.

Shake garlic cloves vigorously in a jar to quickly remove their skins.

Blot tomato slices with kitchen towel to prevent soggy sandwiches.

Treat herbs like flowers – place cut stems in a cup of water and store in the fridge to extend their life.

When grilling fish on a barbecue, place it on top of sliced lemons to prevent sticking and add extra flavour.

Rescue burnt biscuits by gently grating off the burnt edges.

Slice cherry tomatoes quickly by sandwiching them between two plates and cutting in one motion.

Freeze Parmesan rinds and add them to stews or Bolognese for a richer flavour.

Save vegetable cooking water to use as a base for gravy.

Grate frozen butter for easier incorporation into pastry.

Keep pastry cool: turn off the heating, open windows, and plunge your hands into ice-cold water before starting.

Microwave lemons and limes for a few seconds to maximise juice extraction.

Test egg freshness by placing it in water – fresh eggs sink, while stale ones float or stand upright.

Older eggs are easier to peel when making hard-boiled eggs.

Use a hand mixer to whip up light, fluffy mashed potatoes.

Don't be afraid of buying precooked rice pouches or ready-made puff pastry.

Family FAVOURITES

In this chapter you will find recipes I turn to time and time again to keep everyone at the table satisfied. They are the kind of meals that I know hit the mark and are met with genuine gratitude. There is no greater reward than a heartfelt 'thanks mum' from the boys and these recipes never fail to bring that moment of joy. My boys are both over 16 now, but when they were growing up these meals were things that both adults and children would enjoy equally. For younger children, these recipes are easy to adjust – just add chilli or herbs right at the end for a bit of adult-friendly flair.

Pulled BBQ Pork

Pork shoulder is an affordable cut bursting with flavour when cooked low and slow.
This pulled pork is beautifully smoky, sticky, and sweet – a versatile dish you can
serve in countless ways.

Preparation time – 10 minutes
Cooking time – 3.5 hours
Serves 4

For the marinade

2 cloves of garlic, minced

1 tbsp ketchup

1 tbsp Worcestershire sauce

1 tbsp soy sauce

2 tsp smoked paprika

1 tsp ground cumin

1 tbsp honey

1 tsp chilli flakes (optional)

Salt and pepper

For the pork

500-600g boneless, skinless pork shoulder

2 red onions, sliced

100ml chicken stock

5 spring onions, finely chopped

Fresh coriander, to serve

Preheat the oven to 180°C fan/200°C conventional.

Mix all the ingredients for the marinade together and coat the pork thoroughly. Add the onions to the bottom of a snug oven dish. Place the pork on top and season generously. Pour the stock in the bottom of the pan. Cover with foil and cook in the oven for 30 minutes before turning the heat down to 160°C fan/180°C conventional. Cook for another 2.5 hours, remove the foil, baste with the juices and cook for another 20 to 30 minutes or until tender. Allow to rest before pulling apart with two forks and mixing in with the juices at the bottom of the pan.

Finish with spring onions and coriander.

Serve with mashed potatoes, polenta or in baked potatoes with a green salad.

Tip

Make extra and serve the following day in pulled pork buns, or with cheese inside quesadillas. This is also a great one for your slow cooker: simply cook for 4 hours on high.

Sticky Mango Chutney Chicken

This is a wonderful way to introduce children to mild spices – the cumin brings warm flavour without heat, and the mango chutney adds a sweet, sticky touch. When mine were younger, I'd leave out the chilli and add it later to the adult portions for extra kick. Feel free to do the same!

Preparation time – 10 minutes, plus 30 minutes marinating
Cooking time – 30 minutes
Serves 4

For the marinade

2 tbsp mango chutney
Juice of ¼ a lemon
1 tbsp olive oil
1 tsp ground cumin
Salt and pepper

For the chicken

8 chicken thigh fillets
1 red chilli, finely sliced
Lemon wedges, to serve
Chopped fresh coriander, to serve

Mix the marinade ingredients together and add the chicken. Leave for 30 minutes.

Preheat the oven to 180°C fan/200°C conventional.

Place the chicken on a lined baking sheet. Sprinkle with chilli and season with salt and pepper, then cook in the oven for 30 minutes.

Be sure to spoon over the juices, and serve alongside a green salad and basmati rice.

Serve with lemon wedges and coriander.

Philly Steak Sandwich

When I was touring as a dancer back in '94, a stop in Philadelphia introduced me to a sandwich I've never forgotten. It was thanks to a local cast-mate taking us Brits around the Museum of Art that I experienced my first taste of Philly's iconic sandwich, inspiring this version decades later.

Preparation time – 15 minutes
Cooking time – 30 minutes
Serves 4

4 Bavette steaks
2 tbsp mayonnaise
1 clove of garlic, crushed
2 onions, finely sliced
2 red peppers, finely sliced
4 large sub rolls
8 slices provolone cheese
Salt and pepper
Oil

Start by seasoning the steak generously.

Mix the garlic and mayonnaise together and set aside.

Sauté the onions in a pan until golden. Add the peppers, season with salt and pepper and continue to cook until the peppers are tender.

Cook the steaks in a hot pan for 3 minutes on each side. Remove from the pan and allow to rest for 10 minutes.

Slice the sub rolls in half and toast on each side. You can do this in the steak pan for extra flavour if you like.

Slice the steak as thinly as possible and stir through the onions and peppers. Add any juices from the plate too. Keeping the pan on a low heat, add the cheese on top to melt. Once melted, spread the garlic mayonnaise on the rolls. Share the mixture between the rolls and serve immediately.

Cajun Prawn Tacos with Avocado and Mango Salsa

Don't you just love it when a quick and easy meal tastes fantastic? Well, these amazing tacos are a real crowd-pleaser and perfect for an easy after work meal.

Preparation time – 15 minutes
Cooking time – 10 minutes
Serves 4

350g raw tiger prawns
8 small soft tacos

For the marinade

2 tsp Cajun spice mix
½ tsp chipotle chilli flakes
1 tbsp olive oil
Juice of ½ a lime
1 tsp honey
Salt and pepper

For the salsa

1 avocado, chopped into small chunks
1 small mango, peeled and finely diced
½ red onion, finely chopped
10 cherry tomatoes, finely chopped
Juice of ½ a lime
1 tbsp olive oil
Salt and pepper
Fresh chilli, finely chopped (optional)

For the quick pickled onions

1 small red onion, finely sliced
100ml white wine vinegar
80ml water
½ tsp sugar
½ tsp salt

To serve

3 spring onions, finely chopped
Lime wedges, to serve
Sour cream (optional)

For the quick pickled onions, slice the red onion and cover with the white wine vinegar, water, sugar and salt. Leave to pickle for 15 minutes.

Mix the marinade ingredients together and add the prawns. Leave for 5 minutes. Pan fry in a medium to hot pan until they are pink on each side and cooked through.

Mix the salsa ingredients together in a bowl.

Toast the tacos in a dry frying pan and shape in an upside-down muffin tin.

Share the ingredients equally between the tacos and serve immediately with the pickled onions, spring onions, lime wedges and sour cream on the side.

Tip

While you focus on the prawns, delegate someone to be on taco toasting duty.

Miso Chicken Poke Bowls

I can't imagine cooking without miso paste now – it's a star ingredient in many recipes throughout my repertoire. Miso poke bowls are a standout dinner: balanced, delicious, and a feast for the eyes.

Preparation time – 15 minutes, plus 20 minutes to marinate
Cooking time – 30 minutes
Serves 4

For the marinade

2 tsp miso paste

2 tbsp soy sauce

½ tbsp sesame oil

1 tbsp honey

For the dressing

1 clove of garlic, crushed

1 tsp grated ginger

3 tbsp soy sauce

Juice of 1 lime

1 tbsp sesame oil

2 tsp honey

Salt and pepper

For the poke bowl

4 skinless, boneless chicken breasts

500g jasmine rice, cooked

250g frozen edamame beans, steamed

½ cucumber, peeled and sliced

250g mango, peeled and chopped

1 avocado, sliced

4 spring onions, sliced

1 red chilli, sliced (optional)

Sesame seeds, to serve (optional)

Mix the marinade ingredients together in a bowl and set aside. Add all the dressing ingredients to a jar, shake and set that aside too.

Preheat the oven to 180°C fan/200°C conventional.

Add the chicken breasts to the marinade and coat thoroughly. Leave for 20 minutes.

Place the chicken on a baking sheet and season with salt and pepper, then cook in the oven for 25 to 30 minutes. Remove from the oven and allow to rest for 5 minutes before slicing.

To assemble, fill the bowls with rice, then add the edamame, cucumber, mango, avocado and spring onions in separate sections of the bowl so they don't mix. Place the sliced chicken on top. Sprinkle with sliced chilli and sesame seeds if using, and drizzle generously with the dressing.

Feast with your eyes, and enjoy.

Tip

You can make the marinade and coat the chicken up to 24 hours before cooking. Alternatively, you can freeze the chicken breasts in the marinade and store them in the freezer for up to 3 months. Defrost slowly overnight in the fridge before cooking.

Spiced Honey Glazed Chicken Skewers with Greek Salad Salsa

This bright recipe elevates simple chicken thighs into something memorable. On sunny days, these skewers are perfect for the barbecue. Just grill them on low to medium heat and watch closely, as the marinade can char easily.

Preparation time – 15 minutes, plus 30 minutes marinating

Cooking time – 30 minutes

Serves 4

8 chicken thigh fillets

For the marinade

2 cloves of garlic, crushed

2 tsp ground cumin

1 tsp smoked paprika

½ tsp oregano

Juice of ½ a lemon

1 tbsp olive oil

1 tbsp honey

For the Greek salad salsa

¾ cucumber, peeled and chopped

8 cherry tomatoes, finely chopped

1 small red onion, finely chopped

6-8 black olives, roughly chopped

½ block of feta, crumbled

Juice of ½ a lemon

2 tbsp olive oil

½ tsp dried oregano

Salt and pepper

Mix together all the ingredients for the marinade and coat the chicken thoroughly. Leave for 30 minutes. While the chicken is marinating, preheat the oven to 180°C fan/200°C conventional.

Thread the chicken onto the skewers and place on a baking sheet lined with parchment paper. Cook in the oven for 30 minutes.

In a bowl, mix together the ingredients for the Greek salad salsa and set aside.

When the skewers are done, spoon over the salsa, and serve with rice or flatbreads.

Tip

If you want to use chicken breasts, cut them into cubes before threading onto skewers and cook in the oven for just 20 minutes. These also make the most delicious lunch cold, when you have leftovers and are on the go the next day.

Chicken and Mushroom Pot Pie

These tasty, comforting pies are not only a joy to eat, but they are a great thing to batch cook for your fridge or freezer. A hit with the whole family and the perfect midweek meal.

Preparation time – 15 minutes
Cooking time – 60 minutes
Makes 4 pies

2 onions, finely chopped
3 cloves of garlic, crushed
8-10 chicken thigh fillets, each chopped into 3
50g butter
50g plain flour
500ml milk
250ml chicken stock
200g chestnut mushrooms, quartered
1 tbsp chopped tarragon leaves
375g ready-rolled puff pastry
1 egg, beaten (as egg wash)
Salt and pepper

Sauté the onion until soft and sweet, then add the garlic. Add the chicken to the pan and season with salt and pepper. Cook for about 6 minutes so that the chicken is nearly cooked through. Add the butter and melt while stirring. Sprinkle in the flour and fully incorporate into the chicken mixture. Slowly add the milk, stirring to get rid of any lumps. Now add the stock, stir and bring to a gentle simmer. Stir in the mushrooms and tarragon, cover with a lid on and simmer on the hob for 15 minutes on a low heat, stirring here and there to prevent the sauce from sticking.

Taste the sauce and season, if needed. Distribute the filling between 4 pie dishes and allow to cool completely.

Unroll the pastry, cut out 4 rounds the same size as your pie dishes and top each pie with a lid, using a little of the egg wash to help the lid to stick. Score with a sharp knife in a diamond pattern and brush with egg. Poke a little hole in the lids to allow the steam to escape.

Preheat the oven to 180°C fan/200°C conventional and cook the pies in the oven for 30 to 40 minutes or until the pastry is golden and the filling is piping hot.

Tip
Be sure to allow the filling to cool completely before adding the pastry lid or the pastry will start to melt and not puff up beautifully. If you have excess pastry, why not cut out the initials of the pie eater and add them to the lid?

Sausage Plait

Imagine this as a giant, extra-tasty sausage roll – perfect for a simple, budget-friendly meal. I love it with a leafy green salad tossed in lemon and olive oil, but if you're feeling nostalgic, serve it up with baked beans and chips for a classic touch!

Preparation time – 20 minutes
Cooking time – 25-30 minutes
Serves 4

400g sausage meat
1 onion, finely chopped
1 tbsp chopped parsley
1 sheet of ready-rolled puff pastry
1 egg, beaten (as egg wash)
Olive oil

Sauté the onion in olive oil until soft. Set aside and allow to cool.

Preheat the oven to 180°C fan/200°C conventional.

In a bowl, mix the onion and parsley into the sausage meat until fully incorporated. You may need to use your hands. Unroll the pastry, leaving it on the parchment paper, and place it in front of you so that it's portrait.

Form the sausage meat into a log shape and place vertically in the middle of the pastry – there should be at least 5cm of space between the sausage and the edge. Using a sharp knife, make a cut from the corner of the pastry to the corner of the sausage meat, diagonally. Make diagonal cuts along each side of the sausage meat, about 3cm apart, to the edge of the pastry. It should look a little like the veins of a leaf. Fold over the bottom and top flaps of pastry onto the sausage meat and brush with egg wash. Now alternate the diagonal strings bringing them in and on top of the sausage meat to create a plait effect.

Brush with egg wash, place on a baking tray and cook in the oven for 25 to 30 minutes or until golden and cooked through.

Remove from the oven and cool for 5 minutes before slicing.

Tip

This is something you can make in advance and store in the fridge, ready to cook as and when you need it. It also freezes well but will need to be defrosted slowly overnight in the fridge before cooking.

Three Cheese Mac and Cheese with Breadcrumb Topping

Mac and cheese is the ultimate comfort food, loved by all ages. I've used three cheeses here – Parmesan and cheddar for rich flavour, and mozzarella for a wonderful texture and that all-important cheese pull!

Preparation time – 10 minutes

Cooking time – 1 hour

Serves 4

300g dried macaroni

50g butter

1½ tbsp plain flour

500ml milk

4 cloves of garlic, crushed

150g grated Parmesan

150g grated cheddar

1 ball of mozzarella, sliced into pieces and drained on kitchen paper

2 tbsp breadcrumbs

Olive oil

Salt

Start by bringing a pan of salted water to the boil for the macaroni.

In a separate pan, melt the butter on a low heat. Add the flour and stir to make a roux. Cook for 2 minutes while stirring the whole time. Gradually add the milk and continue to stir until you have a smooth sauce. Add the garlic and keep on lowest heat and bring to a simmer. Continue to stir while the sauce thickens.

Preheat the oven to 180°C fan/200°C conventional.

Cook the macaroni for 2 minutes less than the packet instructions state. Drain.

Once the sauce has thickened, add three quarters of the Parmesan and all the cheddar, then when melted add the macaroni and stir to combine.

Pour into an oven dish and nestle the mozzarella throughout the dish. Sprinkle with the breadcrumbs and the remaining Parmesan. Drizzle with a little olive oil and cook in the oven until golden and bubbling.

Tip

To take it up a notch, drizzle with a little truffle oil. This can be made as one big dish or several individual dishes.

Special Egg Fried Rice

Although it makes a fantastic side, this dish is designed to be a meal in itself. Packed with goodies from every food group, it's a perfect midweek solution for busy days, transforming simple ingredients into a satisfying, wholesome plateful.

Preparation time – 15 minutes
Cooking time – 15 minutes
Serves 4

150g bacon lardons
150g raw prawns
4 cloves of garlic, crushed
1 tsp grated ginger
200g sugar snap peas, chopped
4 spring onions, sliced
2 packets of microwave jasmine rice, cooked and cooled
2 eggs, beaten
1 tbsp sesame oil
1 tbsp mirin
1-2 tbsp soy sauce

Add the bacon to a pan and sauté until golden. Add the prawns, garlic, ginger, sugar snaps and spring onions. Cook for 4 minutes or until the prawns are pink. Stir through the cold cooked rice and warm through. Push the rice to the side and scramble the eggs in the centre of the pan, then stir to combine. Add the sesame oil, mirin and soy sauce and continue stirring. Serve immediately.

Sausage Pasta

My boys have grown up enjoying a bowl of this at least twice a month their whole lives. It's economical to make and totally delicious to eat.

Preparation time – 10 minutes
Cooking time – 60 minutes
Serves 4

Olive oil
3-4 small onions, finely chopped
5 cloves of garlic, crushed
6 good quality lean sausages
100ml red wine
2 tins of chopped tomatoes, *or* 800g passata
1 tbsp tomato purée
400g dried pasta
Parmesan cheese, grated (optional)
Salt and pepper

Heat some olive oil in a pan, add the onions and season with salt and pepper. Cook low and slow until they start to caramelise, then add the garlic. With kitchen scissors, chop the sausages into the pan and stir them into the onion mixture to get a little colour. Be careful not to burn the onions. Turn the heat to high and pour in the wine, then let it reduce. Add the tinned tomatoes, stir, and simmer on a low heat with the lid on for 45 to 60 minutes. Once the flavours are married, add the tomato purée and cook uncovered for 10 minutes.

Cook the pasta according to the packet instructions. Toss with the sauce and serve. Add grated Parmesan if you wish.

Tip

Use the best quality sausages you can afford and spend a little time sautéing the onions until soft and golden for a rich and delicious sauce. The red wine adds depth of flavour but only if you have a bottle open. I've made this plenty of times without and it's still lovely.

Bacon and Leek Pasta Bake

When planning my weekly meals, I love to include a few budget-friendly recipes.
These are often comforting, carb-based dishes using ingredients I already have
tucked away in the cupboard or fridge. Bacon and crème fraîche last well, and the
rest is usually close at hand – simple, satisfying, and economical.

Preparation time – 15 minutes
Cooking time – 45 minutes
Serves 4

400g dried pasta

200g chopped bacon *or* bacon lardons

3 medium leeks, washed and finely chopped

4 cloves of garlic, crushed

100ml chicken stock

400g crème fraîche

1 ball of mozzarella, drained, patted dry and
roughly chopped

4 tbsp grated Parmesan *or* strong cheddar

2 tbsp dried breadcrumbs

Salt

Preheat the oven to 180°C fan/200°C conventional.

Cook the pasta in salted water for 2 minutes less than the packet
instructions state.

Add the bacon to a pan and sauté until golden. Add the leeks and
garlic, season and cook until soft.

Pour in the stock and cook for 5 minutes. Stir through the crème
fraîche, warm it through and then stir to combine.

Drain the pasta and stir it into the sauce.

Transfer everything to an oven dish and dot the mozzarella around
it. Sprinkle with half the cheese, then the breadcrumbs, followed by
the rest of the cheese. Cook it in the oven until golden and bubbling,
approximately 20 minutes.

Serve hot.

Tip

If you want you want to get ahead, prepare the recipe until just
before baking. Cool, cover with foil and cook when needed.

Prawn and Pea Orzo

Prawns and peas make a wonderfully sweet duo, perfect in this creamy pasta that's sure to win over the whole family. Ready in just under 30 minutes, it's an ideal dish for busy evenings – a comforting crowd-pleaser that's as quick as it is delicious.

Preparation time – 5 minutes
Cooking time – 20 minutes
Serves 4

2 small onions, finely chopped
3 cloves of garlic, crushed
600ml crème fraîche
300-350g raw prawns
350g frozen peas (I like petits pois)
1 tbsp finely chopped dill
400g dried orzo
Extra virgin olive oil, to serve
Pea shoots, to serve (optional)

Sauté the onions until soft and sweet, then add the garlic and cook for 1 minute. Pour in the crème fraîche and warm through on a low heat. Add the prawns, peas and dill and cook on the lowest heat for 10 minutes or until pink.

Bring a pan of salted water to the boil and cook the orzo according to the packet instructions. Drain the orzo once cooked, making sure to save some of the pasta water.

Toss the pasta through the sauce, gradually adding a little pasta water to loosen. Finish with a drizzle of extra virgin olive oil and pea shoots.

Tip

If you want to get ahead, set aside some time in advance to have everything chopped and portioned ready to go for a super quick meal.

Creamy Bacon and Mushroom Pasta

I've made this cosy pasta dish for years, sometimes with crème fraîche, other times with sour cream or single cream (using a bit less of that one). Just before serving, I add a fresh herb – coriander, chives, chervil, basil, or parsley. It's a reliable, crowd-pleasing dish for hungry mouths.

Preparation time – 15 minutes
Cooking time – 30 minutes
Serves 4

1 large onion, finely chopped
200g bacon lardons
3-4 cloves of garlic, crushed
300g chestnut mushrooms, chopped
100ml white wine
500ml crème fraîche
400g dried pasta
Parmesan and fresh herbs, to serve
Salt

Bring a pot of salted water to the boil and cook the pasta according to the packet instructions. Save some of the cooking water to loosen your sauce.

While the pasta is cooking, sauté the onion until soft. Add the bacon and garlic and cook until golden. Throw in the mushrooms and cook for approximately 5 minutes. Pour in the wine and reduce the heat, stirring through the crème fraîche while on low. Add in the cooked pasta and as much of the cooking water as you need to get the desired consistency. Finish with grated Parmesan and your herb of choice.

Speedy DINNERS

Whether you're a busy professional or juggling life as a parent, time is often in short supply. On those nights when dinner needs to come together fast, these recipes are your answer. Quick to cook with minimal prep, they don't compromise on flavour or elegance. In fact, many of these dishes have even graced my dinner table when entertaining friends – because let's face it, spending time with your guests matters just as much as the meal itself.

Sirloin Steak with Asian-style Chimichurri

This tasty combo is quick to prepare and works with any cut of steak – perfect to keep in mind for barbecue season. The chimichurri sauce is absolutely addictive, so making a double batch isn't just smart, it's essential, as you'll all be reaching for more!

Preparation time – 10 minutes
Cooking – 20-25 minutes
Serves 2

2 sirloin steaks
Oil
Salt and pepper
5 cloves of garlic, whole

For the chimichurri

1 clove of garlic
1 small bunch of coriander
1 red *or* green chilli
1 tsp grated ginger
½ tsp ground cumin
1 tbsp sesame oil
Juice of ½-1 lime
½ tbsp soy sauce
1-2 tsp honey
Salt and pepper

For the garnish

Red chilli, sliced
Lime wedges
Fresh coriander

Start by making the chimichurri. Blitz all the ingredients in a mini chopper or Nutribullet, and set aside.

For a medium rare, thick-cut steak, preheat a large frying pan until smoking.

Drizzle the steak in a little oil and season generously. Once the pan is hot, add the steak, fat side down. Hold with tongs until the fat is golden and crisp. Pan fry on each side for 2½ minutes, throwing in the garlic at the same time. Switch off the heat and keep the steak in the pan for another 1½ minutes on each side, letting the residual heat continue the cooking process. Remove from the pan and allow to rest for 15 minutes before serving.

Carve and drizzle with the chimichurri and garnish with sliced chilli, fresh coriander and lime wedges.

Tip

This Asian-inspired twist on chimichurri is also delicious with chicken, fish, prawns, grilled halloumi, tofu and roasted vegetables.

Chicken Koftas with Tzatziki

Juicy chicken koftas with cool, refreshing tzatziki bring a taste of the Mediterranean to summer. Delicious cooked on a barbecue, these spiced bites that invite everyone to dip, wrap, and savour make a perfect dish for gathering and sharing.

Preparation time – 20 minutes
Cooking time – 30 minutes
Serves 4

For the chicken kofta

500g chicken mince
1 small red onion, finely chopped or grated
2 cloves of garlic, crushed
1 egg
50g breadcrumbs
2 tsp ground cumin
½ tsp dried oregano
2 tbsp finely chopped fresh coriander
Salt and pepper

For the tzatziki

1 small cucumber *or* ½ a regular cucumber
4 tbsp Greek yoghurt
3 cloves of garlic, crushed
1 tbsp finely chopped mint leaves
1 tbsp finely chopped fresh coriander
1-2 tsp extra virgin olive oil

Preheat the oven to 180°C fan/200°C conventional.

In a bowl, mix all the kofta ingredients together with your hands. Once mixed, shape them into sausages and thread onto skewers. 3 should fit on each skewer.

Place on a baking sheet and cook in the oven for 25 to 30 minutes.

To make the tzatziki, coarsely grate the cucumber and squeeze as much water out as possible with a clean tea towel. Mix with the rest of the tzatziki ingredients and check the seasoning.

Remove the koftas from the oven and serve with flatbreads, salad and tzatziki.

Tips

If you want to get ahead then they will sit happily raw in the fridge for 24 hours or can be frozen for 3 months. Remove from the freezer and defrost slowly overnight in the fridge before cooking.

If cooking on a barbecue, oil the grill before adding the koftas to prevent them sticking and don't be tempted to turn them prematurely or too often.

Thai Beef Noodle Salad

Vibrant and fresh, this Thai beef salad combines tender beef with crisp vegetables and tangy dressing. It's a perfect balance of savoury and zesty flavours, all wrapped up with noodles to create a delicious yet complete meal. This is a great dish that brings a burst of Thai-inspired flavours to any table.

Preparation time – 15 minutes
Cooking time – 5 minutes, plus resting
Serves 2

For the dressing

2 cloves of garlic, crushed
1 tsp grated ginger
Juice of 1-2 limes
3 tbsp fish sauce
2 tbsp sesame oil
1 tbsp honey
1 red chilli, finely chopped
Salt and pepper

For the salad

2 sirloin steaks
275-300g dried noodles
2 baby gem lettuce, leaves separated
10-12 cherry tomatoes
1 banana shallot, finely sliced
½ cucumber, peeled, deseeded, halved lengthways, and sliced
1 tbsp chopped fresh mint
1 tbsp chopped fresh coriander
2 tbsp peanuts, *or* cashews

Shake the dressing ingredients together in a jar and set aside.

For a medium rare, thick-cut steak, preheat a large frying pan until smoking.

Drizzle the steak in a little oil and season generously. Once the pan is hot, add the steak, fat side down. Hold with tongs until the fat is golden and crisp. Pan fry on each side for 2½ minutes, throwing in the garlic at the same time. Switch off the heat and keep the steak in the pan for another 1½ minutes on each side, letting the residual heat continue the cooking process.

Remove from the pan and allow to rest while you assemble the salad.

Cook the noodles according to the packet instructions. Drain and drizzle in a little sesame oil to stop them from sticking. Toss the salad ingredients together with half the dressing.

Thinly slice the steaks and place on top of the salad. Drizzle with the remaining dressing, and serve.

Tip

If you want a try a more authentic experience, then be brave and use a few Thai chillies in the dressing. If you'd rather something a little milder, then stick to a fat red chilli.

This salad is a great way to use leftover roast beef, chicken, pork or lamb from a Sunday roast.

Salmon Tikka Skewers with Green Chutney

These salmon tikka skewers are a vibrant twist on a classic, with succulent salmon marinated in aromatic spices and baked to perfection. Paired with a refreshing green chutney, they make a flavourful and eye-catching dish – perfect for gatherings or a fun, flavour-packed meal at home.

Preparation time – 10 minutes
Cooking time – 10 minutes
Serves 4

500g salmon fillets, cut into large chunks
½ red onion, sliced
Coriander leaves, to serve

For the marinade

½ tsp salt
2 cloves of garlic, crushed
2 tsp grated ginger
1 tsp smoked paprika
1 tsp ground cumin
1 tsp ground coriander
½ tsp ground turmeric
3 tbsp olive oil
1 red chilli

For the green chutney

1 clove of garlic
1 small bunch of coriander
1 green chilli
½ tsp ground cumin
Juice of ½ a lemon
2 tsp honey
2-3 tbsp olive oil
Salt and pepper

Preheat the oven to 180°C fan/200°C conventional.

Mix the ingredients for the marinade together and coat the salmon thoroughly. Leave for 5 minutes.

Blitz the green chutney ingredients together in a mini chopper.

Thread the salmon on to skewers and place on a baking sheet lined with parchment paper. Season with salt and pepper and cook in the oven for 10 minutes.

Remove from the oven and drizzle with the chutney, then scatter with the sliced red onion and coriander leaves to serve.

Tip

This amazing green chutney is divine and it's definitely worth making extra to jazz up simple ingredients. This will keep for 3 days in the fridge.

Asian Crab Cakes

These Asian-style crab cakes showcase the delicate sweetness of crab with a touch of spice for balance. Golden and crisp on the outside with a tender interior, they are perfect for a light supper, or as a showstopping starter at any dinner party.

Preparation time – 10 minutes
Cooking time – 10 minutes
Serves 2, as a main, or 4, as a starter

200g white crab meat
$\frac{1}{2}$-1 red chilli, finely chopped
4 spring onions, finely chopped
1 tbsp finely chopped fresh coriander
1 clove of garlic, crushed
1 tsp grated ginger
1 egg
2-3 tbsp panko breadcrumbs
Olive oil
Salt and pepper
Lime wedges, to serve

In a bowl, combine all of the ingredients except the olive oil, salt, pepper and lime, adding extra panko breadcrumbs if it feels too wet. Using your hands, squeeze the mixture into 4 patties approximately 1 inch thick.

On a medium-high heat, preheat a nonstick pan with a little olive oil. Season the crab cakes with salt and pepper, then add the crab cakes to the pan and cook until golden. Try not to move them around too much. Carefully turn with one quick movement – I find a silicone spatula works well here. When golden on both sides and hot all the way through, serve immediately.

Tip
It's imperative to use a good nonstick pan here and don't be tempted to turn the crab cakes prematurely. Give them a chance to colour and create a golden crust before turning once.

Salmon and Dill Fish Cakes with Tartare Sauce

These fish cakes are a clever way to use up leftovers – perfect for extra poached salmon or mashed potatoes. They're just as tasty with tinned salmon, so you can enjoy a delicious, resourceful meal without any fuss.

Preparation time – 15 minutes
Cooking time – 10 minutes
Serves 4

For the fish cakes

300g skinless salmon fillets

Juice of ½ a lemon

2 tsp honey

Salt and pepper

450g mashed potato (use leftovers or cheat and buy instant)

5 spring onions, finely chopped

2 tbsp finely chopped fresh dill

3 tbsp plain flour

1 egg, beaten

80g breadcrumbs

Lemon wedges, to serve

Olive oil

For the tartare sauce

3 tbsp mayonnaise

1 banana shallot, finely chopped

2 tbsp capers, roughly chopped

3 cornichons, finely chopped

Preheat the oven to 180°C fan/200°C conventional.

Add the salmon to an oven dish, squeeze over the lemon juice and drizzle with the honey. Season with salt and pepper and cook in the oven for 10 minutes. Remove from the oven and leave to cool on some kitchen towel.

Mix the potato, spring onions and dill together and season with salt and pepper.

Flake the salmon into small chunks and combine with the potato. Using your hands, form into 8 patties. Dust each one with flour, dip into the beaten egg and then coat in breadcrumbs.

Shallow fry the fish cakes in olive oil until they are golden on each side and warmed through. You may need to do this in batches.

For the tartare sauce, mix the ingredients in a small bowl and then serve alongside the fish cakes.

Speedy Dinners

Red Thai Prawn Ramen

Who doesn't love a warming bowl of flavourful ramen? This quick, simple and delicious recipe is so easy to make and good fun to eat. Feel free to play around with the vegetables – sugar snaps, baby corn and beansprouts all work well here – and add extra chilli if you like a bit of a kick.

Preparation time – 15 minutes
Cooking time – 20 minutes
Serves 4

1 onion, finely chopped

2 eggs

4 cloves of garlic, crushed

2 tsp grated ginger

2 tbsp Thai red curry paste

2 tins of coconut milk

500ml vegetable stock

4 nests dried noodles

2 bulbs pak choi, sliced lengthways into quarters

200g edamame beans (I use frozen)

300g raw prawns

1 red chilli, finely sliced

4 spring onions, finely sliced, to serve

Lime wedges, to serve

Oil

Sauté the onion until soft and at the same time boil the eggs in a separate pan for 6 to 7 minutes. Add the garlic, ginger and red curry paste to the onions and stir to combine. Pour in the coconut milk and stock and simmer on a low heat to let the flavours infuse for 10 minutes.

Toss in the noodles, pak choi, edamame and prawns, bring back to a simmer and cook until the noodles are soft and the prawns are pink. Peel the eggs and cut each in half.

Serve in bowls and finish with half an egg, fresh chilli, spring onion and lime wedges.

Fish Puttanesca

This easy fish puttanesca is a beginner-friendly recipe with all the vibrant flavours of the Mediterranean. With rich tomato passata, briny olives, capers, and a touch of garlic, it pairs beautifully with tender fish for a delicious meal that's ready in a flash. Perfect for any night of the week!

Preparation time – 10 minutes
Cooking time – 35 minutes
Serves 4

2 small onions, finely chopped
Olive oil
3 cloves of garlic, crushed
5 anchovies, finely chopped
100g olives, roughly chopped
3 tsp capers
Salt and pepper
500g passata
4 pieces of cod, skin removed
Fresh herbs, to serve

Sauté the onions in olive oil until soft and sweet. Add the garlic, anchovies, olives and capers. Season with salt and pepper, stir and cook for 2 minutes. Stir through the passata, bring to a simmer with the lid on and cook on a low heat for 20 minutes. Remove the lid and nestle the fish into the sauce. Place the lid back on and continue to simmer for 10 minutes. Remove the lid and finish with black pepper and fresh herbs.

Tip

If you want to make this in advance, cook the sauce so it's ready to go, then heat up and simply poach the fish in the sauce when you are ready to eat. This sauce can be frozen for 3 months.

Pil Pil Prawns

As you can see, my recipes are all about simplicity. This dish proves that cooking doesn't need to be complicated, or time consuming. By simply combining a few ingredients you can create something truly delicious.

Preparation time – 5 minutes
Cooking time – 7 minutes
Serves 2, as a starter

8-10 raw prawns (shell on or off, your choice)
5-6 cloves of garlic, peeled and sliced
$\frac{1}{4}$ tsp chilli flakes
$\frac{1}{4}$ tsp smoked paprika
Olive oil
Salt and pepper

Sizzle the garlic, paprika and chilli in olive oil for 1 minute before adding the prawns. Cook on both sides until pink. Season with salt and pepper and serve with bread.

Indian Spiced Salmon with Yoghurt and Coriander Sauce

One of my favourite ways to serve salmon, this dish brings elegance and flavour to the table with minimal effort. It's simple to prepare yet tastes wonderfully refined – something you'd be delighted to order in a restaurant but can easily enjoy at home, no fuss needed.

Preparation time – 15 minutes
Cooking time – 14 minutes
Serves 4

4 salmon fillets
1 red chilli, finely chopped

For the marinade

$\frac{1}{2}$ tbsp Greek yoghurt
1 clove of garlic
1 tsp grated ginger
Juice of $\frac{1}{4}$ a lemon
2 tsp ground cumin
1 tsp medium curry powder
$\frac{1}{2}$ tsp smoked paprika
2 tsp honey
Salt and pepper

For the yoghurt and coriander sauce

1 tbsp Greek yoghurt
1 tbsp olive oil
1 tbsp finely chopped fresh coriander
1 green chilli, finely chopped
1 small clove of garlic, crushed
Juice of $\frac{1}{2}$ a lemon
2 tsp honey
Salt and pepper

Preheat the oven to 200°C fan/220°C conventional.

Mix the ingredients for the marinade together and add the salmon. Coat thoroughly and leave for 5 minutes.

Place the salmon on a lined baking sheet, season with salt and pepper and sprinkle with chilli. Cook in the oven for 12 to 14 minutes.

While the salmon is cooking, mix the sauce ingredients together in a bowl. Serve with a leafy green salad and Indian bread.

Parma Ham Wrapped Cod with Spinach Puy Lentils and Vine Roasted Tomatoes

Elegant yet simple, this dish marries together tender cod with the savoury, salty flavours of cured prosciutto, earthy lentils and sweet tomatoes. This is a delicious, hearty dish which happens to be healthy, nutritious and well balanced. It's pulled together in no time at all and full of gorgeous textures and flavours.

Preparation time – 10 minutes
Cooking time – 20 minutes
Serves 2

2 cod fillets
4 slices Parma ham
10-12 cherry tomatoes, on the vine
1 tbsp balsamic vinegar
2 banana shallots, finely chopped
2 cloves of garlic, crushed
250g cooked puy lentils
100ml vegetable stock
1-2 handfuls baby spinach leaves
Salt and pepper
Oil

Preheat the oven to 200°C fan/220°C conventional.

Season the cod and then wrap each fillet in a slice of Parma ham. Place on a lined baking sheet along with the tomato vines. Drizzle the tomatoes with the balsamic and season with salt and pepper.

Roast in the oven for 12 to 14 minutes.

While the fish is roasting, sauté the shallots with salt and pepper until soft and sweet. Add the garlic and pan fry for 1 minute. Add the cooked lentils with the stock and warm through. When hot, add the spinach and let it wilt down for a few minutes. Stir, and season if needed. Spoon a portion of the lentils onto a plate, then top with the cod and the tomatoes. Spoon over any juices from the pan and serve.

Miso Glazed Salmon

This is a stunning fusion of savoury and sweet, with a rich, caramelised glaze that perfectly complements the tender salmon. Not only is it one of my boys' favourites, but it's also a quick, flavour-packed dish, bringing depth and umami flavour that pairs beautifully with rice or greens for a satisfying meal.

Preparation time – 10 minutes
Cooking time – 10 minutes
Serves 4

For the marinade

2 tsp miso paste

1 tbsp honey

2 tbsp soy sauce

2 tsp sesame oil

For the salmon

4 salmon fillets

1 tbsp sesame seeds

4 spring onions, finely chopped

1 red chilli, finely sliced

Salt and pepper

Fresh coriander, to serve

Preheat the oven to 200°C fan/220°C conventional.

Mix the marinade ingredients together in a bowl and add the salmon. Leave for no more than 5 minutes. Place the salmon on a baking tray (it's a good idea to use parchment paper to avoid the salmon sticking) and sprinkle with sesame seeds, spring onion and chilli. Season with salt and pepper and cook in the oven for 10 minutes.

Finish with coriander and serve with jasmine rice or noodles and some green vegetables.

Cajun Fish with Black Bean and Avocado Salsa

Here's another simple way to cook fish to perfection. A lovely marinade keeps it moist and tender as it roasts in the oven. This delicious recipe also works beautifully with haddock, pollock, or hake for an easy, vibrant meal.

Preparation time – 15 minutes
Cooking time – 13 minutes
Serves 2

2 skinless cod fillets

For the marinade

½ tsp ground cumin

½ tsp ground coriander

½ tsp smoked paprika

Juice of ½ a lime

2 tbsp olive oil

2 tsp honey

**For the black bean
and avocado salsa**

1 tin of black beans, drained, rinsed and dried

1 avocado, finely chopped

10 cherry tomatoes, finely chopped

½ red onion, finely chopped

1 red chilli, finely chopped

Juice of 1-2 limes

2-3 tbsp extra virgin olive oil

2 tbsp chopped fresh coriander

Salt and pepper

Preheat the oven to 200°C fan/220°C conventional.

In a bowl, stir together the marinade ingredients and coat the cod thoroughly. Leave for 5 minutes.

Mix the salsa ingredients together, taste and adjust the seasoning if necessary.

Place the cod on parchment paper and drizzle with any remaining marinade. Season with salt and pepper and cook in the oven for 10 to 13 minutes.

Spoon the black bean salsa onto a plate and top with the cod. Serve immediately.

Tip

Make a double batch of the salsa as it makes a delicious packed lunch.

Courgette Fritters with Herby Yoghurt

Light, crisp courgette fritters paired with creamy feta and topped with refreshing herby yoghurt create an irresistible dish. Each bite combines savoury, fresh, and creamy notes, making it a perfect starter or side that's simple yet full of flavour.

Preparation time – 10 minutes
Cooking time – 8 minutes
Serves 2

For the fritters

2 large courgettes
1 tsp ground cumin
100g feta, crumbled
1 tbsp flour, plus extra for dusting
Salt and pepper
Oil, for frying

For the herby yoghurt

2 tbsp Greek yoghurt
1 clove of garlic, crushed
1 tbsp chopped fresh mint *or* coriander
A squeeze of lemon juice
Salt and pepper

Grate the courgettes and squeeze out the water with a clean tea towel or kitchen roll. Remove as much water as possible (the drier the better).

Mix the fritter ingredients together in a bowl. Form into 4 patties, then dust in a little flour and season.

Pan fry in oil until golden; roughly 3 to 4 minutes on each side on a medium heat.

While the fritters are cooking, add all of the ingredients for the herby yoghurt to a small bowl and mix together.

Serve the fritters with yoghurt on the side and enjoy.

Tip

While I've used feta, these fritters are also delicious with Parmesan.

Harissa Cauliflower Steaks with Zhoug, Toasted Almonds and Pomegranate Seeds

Cauliflower absorbs flavours brilliantly, making it the perfect base for this dish. Smoky harissa adds warmth, while zhoug brings a fresh, herby kick. Toasted almonds add crunch, and pomegranate seeds provide a sweet, tangy finish, creating a simple yet satisfying combination of textures and tastes.

Preparation time – 30 minutes

Cooking time – 30 minutes

Serves 4

1 cauliflower, sliced into 1 inch steaks

For the marinade

1-2 tsp harissa

Juice of ½ a lemon

1 clove of garlic, crushed

2 tsp honey, *or* agave syrup

2 tbsp olive oil

Salt and pepper

For the hummus

1-2 cloves of garlic, crushed

1 x 400g jar chickpeas, along with 2 tbsp of the liquid

Juice of ½ a lemon

½ tsp ground cumin

1 tbsp tahini

2-3 tbsp extra virgin olive oil

2 ice cubes

For the zhoug

1 small bunch of coriander

1 small bunch of flat leaf parsley

1-2 green chillies, seeds removed

2 cloves of garlic, crushed

Zest of ½ a lemon

Juice of ½ a lemon

1 tbsp olive oil

2 tsp honey

½ tsp ground coriander

½ tsp ground cumin

¼ tsp ground cardamom

Salt and pepper

To serve

2 tbsp toasted flaked almonds

2-3 tbsp pomegranate seeds

Preheat the oven to 180°C fan/200°C conventional.

Mix the ingredients for the marinade together and coat the cauliflower in the marinade.

Blitz the ingredients for the hummus together and set aside.

Using a sharp knife, finely chop the herbs and chillies. Add to a bowl and stir through the remaining zhoug ingredients. Leave for 30 minutes if you can for the flavours to infuse.

Place the cauliflower steaks onto a lined baking sheet. Season with salt and pepper and cook in the oven for 20 to 30 minutes or until tender.

Spoon a portion of hummus on each plate. Top with the cauliflower steaks, then finish with zhoug, pomegranate seeds and almonds.

Tip

If you want to cheat a little, then buy your favourite shop-bought hummus and make the rest from scratch.

One PAN or POT

It's no secret that the kitchen is my happy place – I find it both calming and therapeutic. That said, I'm not a fan of washing up endless pots and pans. Since becoming a mum, I've enjoyed the challenge of creating recipes that can be made in just one dish. You'd be amazed at what's possible! In this chapter, you'll find fuss-free, flavoursome one-pot meals that are even better because all their ingredients come together in the same pan. It's a great chapter for nervous cooks or young budding chefs, with easy, foolproof recipes perfect for any night of the week.

Peanut and Soy Chicken

Here's a versatile marinade I've used for years, perfect on chicken or pork. I tweak it with spring onion, shallot, or ginger depending on what I have. Though this recipe is for the oven, these chicken thighs are outstanding on the barbecue. Give it a try – you won't be disappointed!

Preparation time – 10 minutes, plus 30 minutes marinating
Cooking time – 45 minutes
Serves 4

8-10 chicken thighs (bone in and skin on)
1 tbsp sesame seeds (optional)
1 chilli, sliced, to serve
2 spring onions, sliced, to serve
Lime wedges, to serve

For the marinade

2 tbsp peanut butter
1 tbsp maple syrup
3 tbsp soy sauce
2 cloves of garlic, crushed
2 spring onions, finely chopped
1 tsp grated ginger
1 red chilli, finely chopped
1 tbsp sesame oil

Preheat the oven to 180°C fan/200°C conventional.

In a large bowl, combine all the ingredients for the marinade and set aside.

Slash the chicken through the skin in 3 places. This allows the marinade to penetrate the chicken and speeds up the cooking process.

Place the chicken in the bowl and mix to coat the chicken thoroughly. Cover and leave to marinate for 30 minutes.

Sprinkle with sesame seeds if using, season with salt and pepper and roast in the oven for 30 to 45 minutes.

Remove from the oven and sprinkle with spring onion and chilli.

Serve with the lime wedges and rice or noodles.

Tip

The chicken can be stored in the marinade in the fridge for 24 hours and frozen in the marinade for 3 months. If you have any leftovers once cooked, then pull the meat off the bone and serve hot or cold in a wrap with plenty of salad.

Chicken Saag

This chicken saag is a beautiful blend of tender chicken and vibrant spinach, gently simmered in aromatic spices. It's a comforting dish that's both flavourful and nourishing, offering a taste of classic Indian flavours that are perfect for a cosy, satisfying meal while still being healthy and nutritious.

Preparation time – 10 minutes
Cooking time – 50 minutes
Serves 4-6

6 chicken breast fillets, chopped into chunks
3 onions, finely chopped
Oil
4 cloves of garlic, crushed
2 tsp grated ginger
2 tsp ground cumin
1 tsp ground coriander
1 tsp garam masala
1 tsp fenugreek leaves (optional)
Salt and pepper
4 medium tomatoes, roughly chopped
1 tbsp tomato purée
200g baby spinach leaves
250ml full-fat Greek yoghurt
Red chilli, sliced, for garnish
Lemon slices, for garnish

Sauté the onions until soft and caramelised. This could take about 30 minutes; the more colour, the more flavour. Add the garlic and ginger and cook for 1 minute. Add all of the spices, stir and cook for another minute.

Season the chicken with salt and pepper and add to the pan, coating in all the flavour. Add the tomatoes and tomato purée then cook on a low heat for 5 minutes or until the chicken is nearly cooked. Add the spinach and cook until the spinach has completely wilted. Turn the heat right down and add the yoghurt. Gently warm through for about 3 minutes. Check the seasoning and serve immediately.

Tip

If you want to get ahead, you can make this curry in advance but without adding yoghurt at the end.. Keep in the fridge for 24 hours or freeze for 3 months. Warm through, add yoghurt and serve.

Roast Cod, Vegetable and Potato Traybake with Salsa Verde

This vibrant, flavourful traybake is wonderfully simple and perfect for anyone new to cooking fish. Many don't realise that fish often needs less cooking time than expected, and roasting thicker fillets in the oven works beautifully to bring out their best texture and taste.

Preparation time – 15 minutes
Cooking time – 55 minutes
Serves 4

250g baby new potatoes

Olive oil

Salt and pepper

1 medium red onion, chopped into 8 wedges

2 red peppers, roughly chopped

2 medium courgettes, cut into chunks

2 handfuls of black olives

4 cod fillets

For the salsa verde

1 clove of garlic

1 small bunch of coriander

1 small bunch of flat leaf parsley

2 tsp capers, drained

3-4 anchovies (from a tin)

Juice of ¼ a lemon

3 tbsp extra virgin olive oil (or more if it needs loosening)

1 tsp honey

Salt and pepper

Preheat the oven to 180°C fan/200°C conventional.

Add the potatoes to a roasting pan, drizzle with olive oil and season with salt and pepper. Cook in the oven for 20 minutes. Remove from the oven and add the onion, peppers, courgettes and olives. Toss with the potatoes, adding a little extra oil and seasoning if necessary. Return to the oven and cook for another 20 minutes.

Bring together the salsa verde ingredients in a mini chopper or Nutribullet and set aside.

Remove the vegetables from the oven and nestle the cod fillets into them. Add 1 teaspoon of the salsa verde to each fillet and coat the top of it. Season with salt and pepper and cook in the oven for the final time for 12 minutes.

Serve on plates and drizzle with the salsa verde.

Tip

If using larger new potatoes then halve or quarter each one depending on their size.

Mushroom and Spinach Gnocchi with Burrata

Ready in 15 minutes, in one pan, and only about £1.40 per person! I love that fresh gnocchi can be pan-fried instead of boiled, soaking up all the extra flavours. With a long shelf life, it's a perfect fridge staple. Have you tried pan-frying gnocchi?

Preparation time – 10 minutes

Cooking time – 15 minutes

Serves 4

1 onion, finely chopped

Olive oil

3 cloves of garlic, crushed

250g chestnut mushrooms, sliced

Salt and pepper

450g fresh gnocchi

1 tsp butter

80g fresh spinach

1 ball of burrata, drained on kitchen towel

Truffle oil, to serve (optional)

Sauté the onion in olive oil until soft, then add the garlic and cook for 2 minutes. Now add the mushrooms and season generously with salt and pepper. Cook until soft. Throw in the gnocchi and the butter, stirring every so often until warm. Add the spinach and cook until wilted, and then check the seasoning is to your liking. Top with the burrata and drizzle with truffle oil, if using, to serve.

Chicken and Orzo Traybake

This chicken and orzo traybake is a warm and comforting dish that brings together tender chicken, sweet caramelised peppers and perfectly cooked orzo in one pan. It's a warm, hearty dish with minimal fuss, perfect for cosy dinners when you want big flavour with little effort.

Preparation time – 15 minutes
Cooking time – 45 minutes
Serves 4

1kg chicken thighs
1 medium onion, chopped
2 cloves of garlic, crushed
2 peppers, chopped
Salt and pepper
Olive oil
250g orzo
350ml stock, hot
1 handful of spinach

Preheat the oven to 190°C fan/210°C conventional.

Place the chicken, onions, garlic and peppers into a large roast tray. Season and drizzle with olive oil, then roast in the oven for 20 minutes.

Remove from the oven and set the chicken aside. Pour in the dry orzo and stir. Add the stock, stir and return the chicken to the pan.

Turn down the heat to 180°C fan/200°C conventional. Return the pan to the oven for 20 to 25 minutes. Remove from the oven and stir through the spinach to wilt in the residual heat, adding a little extra hot stock if it looks too dry.

Tip

If you have a young child who is experimenting with food then this is worth trying out. Take a little portion of the orzo, pull some of the chicken from the bone and place in a little bowl. The sweetness from the peppers and onions makes this one very appealing to many a fussy eater.

Roasted Vegetable and Halloumi Traybake

This recipe highlights the perfect balance of sweet honey, salty halloumi, and caramelised roasted vegetables. The marinade adds a rich, sticky finish, making every bite unforgettable. Whether enjoyed as a main dish or paired with roasted chicken, it's hearty, satisfying, and bound to impress at any table.

Preparation time – 15 minutes
Cooking time – 45 minutes
Serves 2 as a main, or 4 as a side

1 block of halloumi, sliced
2 red onions, cut into wedges
1 sweet potato, peeled and chopped into chunks
5 cloves of garlic
2 red peppers, roughly chopped

For the marinade

2 tsp harissa paste
1 clove of garlic, crushed
Juice of $\frac{1}{4}$ a lemon
3 tbsp olive oil
Salt and pepper

To serve

Honey, to drizzle
Pomegranate seeds
Fresh mint, coriander *or* parsley

Preheat the oven to 180°C fan/200°C conventional.

Add the onions, sweet potato, whole garlic cloves and peppers to a roasting tin.

Mix together all the ingredients for the marinade and drizzle over the vegetables. Toss together, coating the vegetables thoroughly and adding a little extra olive oil if necessary. Season with salt and pepper and roast in the oven for 25 to 30 minutes or until everything begins to caramelise.

Take the dish from the oven, then nestle in the halloumi, coating it in the marinade in the pan. Return to the oven and cook for 10 to 15 minutes or until everything is just caramelised.

Remove from the oven and drizzle the halloumi with a little honey. Sprinkle the whole thing with pomegranate seeds and herbs to serve.

Moroccan Fish Tagine

Making this dish for a weekend gathering is always a pleasure. It's simple to prepare yet filled with aromatic spices and vibrant flavours that create an inviting warmth. This dish makes guests feel thoroughly spoilt, bringing a touch of Morocco's rich culinary spirit to your dining room table.

Preparation time – 15 minutes
Cooking time – 45 minutes
Serves 4-6

2 small onions, finely chopped

4 cloves of garlic, crushed

2 tsp grated ginger

1 red chilli, finely chopped

10 cherry tomatoes

2 tsp ground cumin

1 tsp ground coriander

½ tsp ground cinnamon

Pinch of saffron, *or* ½ tsp turmeric

1 tsp harissa

Salt and pepper

4 tsp plain flour

400ml fish stock *or* chicken stock

2 tbsp ground almonds

2 tbsp sultanas

1 tbsp honey

500g white firm fish, chopped into large chunks

2 squid tubes, cleaned and sliced

200g prawns

Salt and pepper

Fresh coriander, to serve

3 tbsp pomegranate seeds, to serve

Oil

Sauté the onions until soft and sweet, then add the garlic, ginger and chilli and fry for 1 minute.

Add the tomatoes, the spices and the harissa along with plenty of salt and pepper and give it a good stir. Spoon in the flour and stir again. Pour in the stock, almonds, sultanas and honey and bring to a gentle simmer for 15 minutes with the lid on.

Pat all of the fish and seafood dry with kitchen towel and season with salt and pepper.

Remove the lid and gently stir the fish into the sauce. Place a lid on and cook on a low-medium heat for 10 to 12 minutes or until the fish is just cooked through.

Top with coriander and pomegranate seeds, and serve with couscous and a green salad.

Tip

If you want to get ahead, you can make the sauce the day before, then simply reheat and poach the fish in the sauce as and when you need it.

Thai Chicken Traybake

This is one of my tastiest and most popular chicken traybakes! The marinade, rich with Thai flavours, pairs beautifully with chicken thighs. Adjust the chilli to your liking, and if you can't find both lemongrass and kaffir lime leaves, no worries, just use what you have on hand.

Preparation time – 10 minutes, plus 20 minutes marinating
Cooking time – 45 minutes
Serves 4

8-10 chicken thighs, skin on
Salt and pepper

For the marinade

2 cloves of garlic, crushed

3 spring onions, finely chopped

1 tbsp grated ginger

2 tbsp fish sauce

2 tbsp soy sauce

1 tbsp sesame oil

2 tbsp maple syrup *or* 1 tbsp honey

1 red chilli, chopped

1 blade of lemongrass, outer tough leaves removed and finely chopped

3 kaffir lime leaves, finely chopped

To serve

Lime wedges

1 chilli, sliced

1 spring onion, sliced

Preheat the oven to 180°C fan/200°C conventional.

Mix the marinade ingredients together in a large bowl, then transfer the chicken to the bowl to marinate. Cover and leave for 20 minutes – or overnight – to soak up all those flavours.

Transfer the chicken skin side up into a roasting pan (along with all the marinade), season with salt and pepper and roast for 35 to 45 minutes.

Serve with lime wedges, sliced chilli, and spring onions alongside rice or noodles and some sugar snap peas for a pop of colour.

Tip

This is a great one to prepare in a larger batch for your freezer. Simply mix the marinade together and add to a large ziplock bag. Add the chicken and massage into the marinade. Freeze for up to 3 months. Defrost slowly overnight and cook when needed.

Oven Baked Prawn and Chorizo Paella

For years, I assumed making paella was too tricky to try at home – until I started baking it in the oven. Paella is a celebration of bold flavours, and while purists might disagree about adding chorizo, I believe that when flavours work this well together, it's worth bending the rules.

Preparation time – 15 minutes
Cooking time – 50 minutes
Serves 4

2 small onions, finely chopped
Oil
5 cloves of garlic, crushed
200g chorizo, sliced
1 tbsp smoked paprika
300g paella rice
125ml white wine
1 litre fish stock *or* chicken stock, hot
Pinch of saffron (optional)
450-500g raw prawns (shell on or off, your choice)
Olive oil
Salt and pepper
Chopped flat leaf parsley, to serve
Lemon wedges, to serve

You will need

1 paella pan, 36cm in diameter
Or
1 shallow casserole dish

Preheat the oven to 180°C fan/200°C conventional.

Place the pinch of saffron into the hot stock to infuse and leave somewhere warm.

Fry the onion in a little oil, and when soft, add the garlic and chorizo. Cook until the oils start releasing from the chorizo, then add the smoked paprika and stir. Add the rice and mix well. Pour in the wine and stir. Now add the hot stock including the saffron to the rice, season generously and carefully stir.

Place it in the oven for 20 minutes.

Remove from the oven and nestle the prawns into the rice, then return to the oven for 10 to 15 minutes. If it's looking a little dry and the rice isn't cooked add a little extra stock and cook for a bit longer.

Finish with parsley and serve with lemon wedges.

Tip

The better your stock, the tastier the paella. An amazing fish or seafood stock will really take this up a notch.

Prawn and Okra Curry

When I'm out for a curry, I almost always choose a prawn dish because it's just too tempting! This prawn and okra curry is no exception. Full of delicate flavours, it's light, healthy, and quick to prepare, combining tender prawns and vibrant okra in a beautifully spiced sauce.

Preparation time – 15 minutes
Cooking time – 50 minutes
Serves 4

2 onions, finely chopped
Oil
4 cloves of garlic, crushed
1 red chilli, finely chopped
2 tsp grated ginger
2 tsp ground cumin
1 tsp medium curry powder
1 tsp garam masala
½ tsp ground turmeric
½ tsp mustard seeds
1 tin of tomatoes
2 tsp honey
150g okra, sliced
300g raw prawns
Fresh coriander, to serve
Lemon wedges, to serve

Sauté the onions until soft, sweet and caramelised. Add the garlic, chilli and ginger and cook for 1 minute. Add the spices, season generously and stir into the onion mixture. Pour in the tomatoes, then fill a third of the tin with water and add that along with the honey and bring to a simmer. Cook on a low heat with the lid on for 20 minutes.

Remove the lid and add the okra. Stir and cook for 5 minutes. Add the prawns and cook for another 5 to 7 minutes or until the prawns are pink.

Serve with basmati rice and finish with coriander and lemon.

Tip

If you want to get ahead, then you can make the sauce and keep it in the fridge for 48 hours or in the freezer for 3 months. Warm through when needed, then add the okra and prawns.

Chicken Shashlik Traybake

After a long day, I'm especially grateful for meals like this. Just toss everything in the pan and let the oven work its magic. The delicious marinade infuses the chicken with rich flavour, and the yoghurt keeps the meat tender and juicy.

Preparation time – 15 minutes, plus 30 minutes for marinating

Cooking time – 45 minutes

Serves 4

800g chicken thighs, skinless and boneless

1 medium red onion, cut into 8 wedges

1 red pepper

1 green pepper

Oil

1 large handful of spinach

For the marinade

2 tbsp Greek yoghurt

3 cloves of garlic, crushed

1 thumb-sized piece of grated ginger

1 red chilli, finely chopped (optional)

2 tsp honey

Juice of ½ a lemon

4 tsp Tandoori spice mix

Or

½ tsp ground cinnamon

2 tsp ground cumin

1 tsp ground coriander

1 tsp smoked paprika

Mix the marinade ingredients together in a bowl and add the chicken. Leave for anywhere between 30 minutes and overnight.

Preheat the oven to 180°C fan/200°C conventional.

Add everything except the spinach to a roasting tin. Drizzle with a little oil and season. Roast for 30 to 45 minutes. If using chicken breasts, cook for no more than 30 minutes. Stir through the spinach and serve.

Tip

This is an excellent one to deliberately make extra of as it makes the most delicious lunch the following day, in flatbreads, wraps and salad bowls.

Roast DINNERS

It's hard to choose a favourite chapter, but I'm particularly proud of this chapter on roasts. Here, you'll find a selection of timeless classics alongside roasts with a modern twist. Some recipes are a labour of love, while others are delightfully simple to prepare.

I hope this chapter becomes one you return to often, offering the perfect excuse to gather loved ones around the table and share a memorable meal together.

Côte de Boeuf

This book would not be complete without sharing my go-to meal when I want to
cook for someone special. It's a combination of classic ingredients that is sure to
bring a smile to many faces. A recipe that should be saved for a special occasion.

Preparation time – 5 minutes
Cooking time – 14-18 minutes
Serves 2

Côte de boeuf (approx. 760g), at room
temperature
4 cloves of garlic, whole
Salt and pepper
Light olive oil

You will need
A large heavy frying pan with a metal handle

Preheat the oven to 180°C fan/200°C conventional.

Drizzle the côte de boeuf with olive oil and season generously with
salt and pepper.

Heat the frying pan over high heat until smoking hot. Add a small
amount of oil to the pan.

Place the beef in the pan and sear for 3 minutes on one side without
moving it to develop a crust. Turn the beef over and repeat on the
other side.

Add the garlic cloves to the pan and transfer it to the oven. Roast for
9 minutes for rare or 13 minutes for medium-rare.

Remove the pan from the oven and turn the beef over. Allow it to rest
in the pan for 10 to 15 minutes before carving.

Asparagus with Lemon and Olive Oil

Preparation time – 5 minutes
Cooking time – 2 minutes
Serves 2

180g fine asparagus, washed and woody ends
removed
Juice of ¼ a lemon
Zest of ½ a lemon
1 tbsp extra virgin olive oil
Salt and pepper
1 handful of shaved Parmesan

Bring a pan of salted water to the boil and add the asparagus. Cover
with a lid and simmer gently for 2 minutes until tender yet crisp.

In a small bowl, whisk together the lemon juice, lemon zest, olive oil,
salt, and pepper.

Drain the asparagus and arrange on a serving plate. Drizzle over the
lemon dressing and scatter with shaved Parmesan.

Roasted New Potatoes with Garlic and Thyme

Preparation time – 10 minutes
Cooking time – 60 minutes
Serves 2

350g new potatoes, chopped into 3cm pieces

5 cloves of garlic, whole

Olive oil

Salt and pepper

3 sprigs of thyme

Preheat the oven to 180°C fan/200°C conventional.

Place the potatoes and garlic in a roasting pan. Drizzle generously with olive oil and season with salt and pepper. Roast in the oven for 50 to 60 minutes, turning at least once during cooking. Add the thyme for the last 10 minutes to infuse the flavours. Serve hot.

Salsa Verde

Preparation time – 5 minutes
Serves 2-4

1-2 cloves of garlic

4 anchovies

1 tsp Dijon mustard

2-3 tbsp extra virgin olive oil

Juice of ½ a lemon

1 tsp honey

Black pepper, to taste

1 small bunch of flat-leaf parsley

1 small bunch of coriander

Combine all the ingredients in a mini chopper and blitz until smooth. Loosen the mixture with extra olive oil if needed. Set aside until ready to serve.

Korean Style Pork Tenderloin

This pork tenderloin is marinated in a bold blend of savoury, sweet and spicy flavours that infuse the meat with richness. Each tender slice is vibrant yet comforting, making this a perfect dish to share and one that's sure to become a favourite.

Preparation time – 15 minutes, plus marinating time
Cooking time – 30 minutes
Serves 4-6

2 whole pork tenderloin/fillets

1 cucumber, shaved into ribbons

2 tbsp sesame seeds

2-3 spring onions, sliced

Lime, to serve

For the dressing

1 red chilli, finely chopped

3 tbsp white condimento *or* white wine vinegar mixed with ½ tsp caster sugar

For the marinade

2 cloves of garlic, crushed

2 tsp grated ginger

2 tbsp ketchup

2 tbsp soy sauce

1 tbsp sesame oil

1 tbsp honey

2 tsp Worcestershire sauce

1-2 tsp sriracha, *or* 1 chilli, finely chopped

Preheat the oven to 200°C fan/220°C conventional.

Mix the marinade ingredients together in a large bowl. Pat the pork dry with kitchen towel and add to the marinade. Leave for 30 minutes or overnight.

Shave the cucumber and pat dry with kitchen roll. Add to a bowl, season and toss with the dressing ingredients.

Place the pork fillets on a lined baking sheet, season generously and sprinkle with sesame seeds (saving some for garnish). Drizzle with oil and roast in the oven for 25 to 30 minutes. Remove from the oven and leave to rest for 15 minutes before carving.

Serve on a platter with the dressed cucumber ribbons and sprinkle with spring onion, sesame seeds and lime juice.

Tip

Pork tenderloin is lean which means it's very quick to cook and can actually be served just blushing. It's really important not to overcook, or it will become dry.

Harissa Leg of Lamb

This roast leg of lamb, infused with harissa, is a true crowd-pleaser. The rich, spicy marinade brings out the lamb's natural flavours as it slowly roasts to tender perfection. It's a dish that feels both comforting and a bit special – a perfect centrepiece for any gathering.

Preparation time – 30 minutes, plus marinating
Cooking time – 1 hour 45 minutes
Serves 6-8

1 leg of lamb, approx. 2.2kg

For the marinade
1 tbsp harissa
2 tsp olive oil
Juice of ½ a lemon
1-2 cloves of garlic, crushed

Preheat the oven to 180°C fan/200°C conventional.

Mix the marinade ingredients together in a bowl.

Slash the lamb in a lattice pattern, approximately 2.5cm apart. Rub the lamb in the marinade and season generously. Leave for 30 minutes.

Roast in the oven for 1 hour to 1 hour 15 minutes for pink, or 1 hour 30 minutes to 1 hour 40 minutes for well done.

Leave to rest for 20 to 30 minutes before carving.

Serve with flatbreads, hummus and a lovely platter of salad ingredients drizzled in lemon, garlic, herbs, olive oil and seasoning.

Roast Sea Bream with Lemon, Shallot and Caper Dressing

This roast offers delicate, tender fish balanced with a bright, tart freshness and subtle sweetness. The dressing adds brininess, gentle richness and tang, lifting the flavours to create a harmonious dish that feels both light and satisfying. Great for a catch from your local fishmonger!

Preparation time – 15 minutes
Cooking time – 20 minutes
Serves 2

For the dressing

1 clove of garlic, crushed

1 shallot, finely chopped

1 tbsp finely chopped dill

2 tsp capers

2 tsp honey

Juice of ½ a lemon

4 tbsp extra virgin olive oil

For the roast sea bream

2 small whole sea bream *or* sea bass, gutted and cleaned

Olive oil

Salt and pepper

Lemon wedges, to serve

Mix the dressing ingredients together in a jar and set aside.

Preheat the oven to 180°C fan/200°C conventional.

Slash the fish 3 times on each side, stopping at the bone. Place the fish on a lined baking sheet. Drizzle 2 teaspoons of the dressing on each side, drizzle with a little extra olive oil and season with salt and pepper. Cook in the oven for 20 minutes.

Remove from the oven, drizzle with the dressing, and serve with a wedge of lemon.

Tip

Make extra dressing and serve it with salmon, chicken or prawns. The dressing will keep in the fridge for 3 days.

Roast Chicken with Fennel, Lemon, Garlic and Tarragon Butter and Tarragon Aioli

The ingredients in this dish come together beautifully, creating a perfect harmony of flavours. As the shallots and onions cook, they turn sticky, caramelised and sweet, leaving a deliciously rich jus at the bottom of the pan that's ready to be savoured.

Preparation time – 15 minutes

Cooking time – 1 hour 30 minutes

Serves 4

1 medium chicken

2 fennel bulbs, tops removed and chopped into wedges with the root intact

4 banana shallots, peeled

200ml vermouth

Salt and pepper

For the lemon, garlic and tarragon butter

2 tbsp butter (room temperature)

3 cloves of garlic, crushed

2 tbsp chopped fresh tarragon

Zest of ½ a lemon

Juice of ½ a lemon

Salt and pepper

For the tarragon aioli

1 large clove of garlic, crushed

1 tbsp chopped fresh tarragon

3-4 tbsp mayonnaise

Preheat the oven to 180°C fan/200°C conventional.

Mix together the ingredients for the lemon, garlic and tarragon butter.

Carefully lift the skin from the neck end of the chicken and slide your hand between the breast and the skin to release the skin. Spread the tarragon butter over the breasts and under the skin, making sure as much is covered as possible.

Add the shallots and fennel to a medium roasting tin, drizzle with olive oil and season with salt and pepper. Sit the chicken on top.

Season the chicken with salt and pepper and roast in the oven for 1 hour. Remove from the oven and pour the vermouth in the bottom of the pan. Remove from the oven and allow to rest for 15 minutes before carving.

Hasselback Roast Butternut Squash

Here's a simple yet flavour-packed way to enjoy butternut squash, a trusty vegetable that keeps well in the fridge. Hasselbacking skips the peeling, speeds up cooking, and lets the harissa infuse every slice. This dish is perfect topped with a little feta or goat's cheese for extra richness.

Preparation time – 15 minutes
Cooking time – 50 minutes
Serves 2 as a main, or 4-6 as a side

1 butternut squash

3 tsp harissa

Oil

1 tbsp tahini

1 tbsp date molasses, *or* balsamic vinegar

2 tbsp pomegranate seeds

1 tbsp flaked almonds

1 tbsp chopped fresh coriander

Preheat the oven to 180°C fan/200°C conventional.

Halve the butternut squash lengthways and scoop out the seeds with a spoon. Place the squash flat side down and with a large sharp knife make slits 2mm apart, being careful not to go all the way through. Coat the squash with harissa, drizzle with oil and season. Place flat side down on a baking tray, cover with foil and roast in the oven for 30 to 45 minutes or 45 to 50 minutes if it's a large squash. Remove the foil for the last 25 minutes.

Remove from the oven and drizzle with tahini and date molasses.

Finish with pomegranate seeds, almonds and coriander.

Whole Roast Salmon with Ginger Chilli and Garlic

This gorgeous dish is a perfect choice for entertaining, combining beautiful presentation with bold flavours. The Asian-inspired marinade enhances the salmon's natural richness, creating a delicious dish that's both impressive and wonderfully simple to make.

Preparation time – 15 minutes
Cooking time – 40 minutes
Serves 8

1 whole salmon (approx. 2kg), gutted
1 thumb-sized piece of ginger, peeled and cut into matchsticks
4 cloves of garlic, finely sliced
2 red chillies, finely sliced
5 spring onions, cut into matchsticks
1 tbsp sesame oil
1 tbsp ground nut oil
2 tbsp soy sauce
Juice of ½ a lime
Lime wedges, to serve

Preheat the oven to 180°C fan/200°C conventional.

Make 3 deep incisions just through to the bone on each side of the fish.

Set aside a third of the garlic, ginger and chilli. Stuff the rest of the ginger, garlic, chilli and spring onion into the cavity, the incisions and also on top of the salmon. Drizzle with both oils, soy sauce and lime juice. Season generously and roast in the oven for 30 to 40 minutes or until cooked through. I cooked mine for 30 minutes and it was just blushing – perfect.

Just before the salmon is cooked, sauté the ginger, garlic and chilli set aside earlier in a little oil for a few minutes until just golden. Sprinkle over the salmon.

Serve with a lime wedge.

Tip

I've made something similar with a large line-caught sea bass – you may need to adjust the timings depending on the size of the fish.

Classic Rib of Beef with Red Wine Gravy and Homemade Horseradish Sauce

This is British cooking at its finest and one of my family's all-time favourite meals. As much as I love a good roast in a country pub, nothing compares to sharing one at home with friends or family. This recipe includes my favourite gravy, perfect with beef.

Preparation time – 15 minutes
Cooking time – 1 hour 40 minutes
Serves 6

1.1kg-1.5kg boneless rib of beef
5 onions, peeled and halved
Salt and pepper

For the gravy

3 shallots *or* 2 red onions, finely chopped
3 cloves of garlic, crushed
3 tsp plain flour
1 tbsp Worcestershire sauce
1 tbsp balsamic reduction
1 tsp soy sauce
125ml red wine
500ml beef stock
Oil

For the horseradish sauce

2 tbsp grated horseradish
2 tbsp crème fraîche
3 tsp mayonnaise
Salt and pepper

Preheat the oven to 210°C fan/230°C conventional.

Season the meat well and place in a roasting tin with the onions. Drizzle with a little oil and place the beef in the oven for 20 minutes, then turn the oven down to 180°C fan/200°C conventional.

Roast the meat for another 40 minutes (for rare) or 50 minutes (for medium-rare) depending on how the steak is preferred.

Leave to rest for 30 minutes before carving.

For the gravy, sauté the shallots or onion in a saucepan with a bit of oil really slowly on a low heat for about 30 minutes until caramelised. Add the garlic and stir for a minute, then introduce the flour and stir into the onions. Mix in the Worcester sauce, balsamic, soy sauce and half of the wine, continuing to stir. Add the stock and allow to simmer on a low heat for 30 minutes, topping up with extra stock or water if necessary.

Drain off most of the fat from the roasting tin. Add the rest of the wine and a little water if required, then simmer and reduce on the hob over a low heat. Stir with a wooden spoon, getting all the flavour from the bottom of the pan.

Pour the roasting pan juices into the gravy. Season and reduce until you have the desired flavour and consistency.

While waiting for the gravy to thicken, add all the ingredients for the horseradish sauce to a bowl and mix.

Serve the beef alongside a generous amount of gravy and a dollop of horseradish sauce and enjoy.

Tip

Be sure to bring your beef joint to room temperature several hours before cooking.

The more colour you get on the onions, the tastier the gravy.

Tandoori Slow-cooked Shoulder of Lamb with Green Chutney

With only 10 to 15 minutes of preparation, this slow-cooked lamb shoulder can be left to gently cook in the oven, filling your kitchen with warm, humble spices. By the time it's ready, the lamb will be perfectly juicy, with tender meat that falls effortlessly off the bone. A must try.

Preparation time – 15 minutes, plus marinating
Cooking time – 6 hours
Serves 4-6

1 shoulder of lamb
2 onions, sliced

For the marinade

3 cloves of garlic, crushed
2 tsp grated ginger
2 tbsp natural yoghurt
Juice of $\frac{1}{2}$ a lemon
2 tsp ground cumin
1-2 tsp chilli powder
1 tsp ground coriander
1 tsp ground turmeric

For the coriander chutney

40g fresh coriander
10g fresh mint
1 green chilli, seeds removed
2 cloves of garlic
1 tsp grated ginger
1 tsp ground coriander
2 spring onions, chopped
Juice of $\frac{1}{2}$ a lemon
2 tsp honey
2 tbsp olive oil
Salt and pepper

Preheat the oven to 140°C fan/160°C conventional.

Mix the marinade ingredients together and coat the lamb thoroughly. Leave for 30 minutes, or overnight.

Sit the lamb on a bed of onions in a snug roasting tray. Cover with foil and place into the oven to cook for 5 to 6 hours, removing the foil for the last hour.

Blend the ingredients for the coriander chutney together until smooth, loosening with extra olive oil if necessary.

Serve the lamb drizzled with the coriander chutney.

Nostalgia RECIPES

This chapter is a tribute to where my love of cooking began. If it weren't for the people and moments celebrated here, my passion for food might never have been sparked. Both my parents shared a deep love for food, and I was lucky to grow up with incredible home cooking. Despite my mum working full-time in the city, she always managed to put a home-cooked meal on the table every evening. In the early days, when Mum and Dad were still together, their dinner parties were legendary – fabulous spreads of delicious dishes, the Bee Gees playing in the background, and my dad ensuring the wine and laughter flowed. Each recipe in this chapter holds a story and stirs a cherished memory, and I'm thrilled to share them with you.

Aubergine Parmigiana

During the late '90s in southern Italy, I fell for the pure beauty of Italian cooking. My then-boyfriend Giuseppe's Nonna made a rich Melanzani Parmigiana, frying each floured aubergine slice. I now opt to roast them – a simpler, equally delicious twist that keeps the heart of the dish alive.

Preparation time – 10 minutes
Cooking time – 40-60 minutes
Serves 4

3 aubergines
Olive oil
1 medium red onion, finely chopped
4-5 cloves of garlic, crushed
500ml passata, *or* tinned tomatoes
1 handful of basil leaves
60g grated Parmesan
180g fresh mozzarella, drained and sliced
Salt and pepper

Preheat the oven to 180°C fan/200°C conventional.

Slice the aubergine lengthways into 1.5cm thick slices. Season with salt and pepper, then sauté in olive oil until golden. Do this in batches and set aside. Alternatively, you can drizzle the aubergine with oil, season and roast for about 20 minutes, turning once in the oven. Fry the onion for 10 minutes until soft, then add the garlic and olive oil and cook for 1 minute. Add the passata and basil and season with salt to taste. Cover and simmer for 15 to 20 minutes on a low heat, then set aside.

Spoon a thin layer of the tomato sauce into an ovenproof dish, then a scattering of Parmesan, followed by a single layer of aubergines and then mozzarella. Repeat these layers until you've used all the ingredients up, finishing with a little sauce and another good sprinkling of Parmesan.

Cook in the oven for 20 to 30 minutes or until golden, then enjoy hot.

My Mum's Chicken in the Brick

Not a week went by without Mum making this for dinner, and if any dish brings me back to childhood, it's this one. Cooking a chicken in a brick (a traditional terracotta pot) creates the most succulent, golden-skinned roast, with every bit of flavour sealed in. The juices at the bottom? Liquid gold – rich, intense, and unforgettable.

Preparation time – 5 minutes
Cooking time – 1 hour 45 minutes, plus 15 minutes resting time
Serves 4

1 lemon, halved
Salt and pepper
1 small chicken
1 bulb garlic

Squeeze half of the lemon juice into the bottom of the brick and season with salt and pepper. Add the chicken to the brick.

Slice the top off horizontally from the garlic bulb. Add all of it to the cavity of the chicken. Squeeze the remaining lemon half over the chicken, then add half of the lemon to the cavity as well. Season with plenty of salt and pepper. Cover with the lid.

Place in a cold oven (this is important!) then turn the heat up to 230°C fan/250°C conventional and cook the chicken for 1 hour 45 minutes.

Carefully remove the chicken from the oven, lift the lid and allow to rest for 15 minutes.

Tip
When serving, be sure to spoon over the juices as it makes the most delicious gravy. Any leftover juices can be kept in the fridge or frozen, and makes a great stock alongside the bones, which can be frozen too!

Veal Milanese

This dish, with its golden, crisp coating and tender bite, was always perfectly paired by Mum with a side of spaghetti. This Italian classic brings elegance to any meal – a comforting dish I still adore, and a childhood favourite I've loved for years.

Preparation time – 10 minutes
Cooking time – 20 minutes
Serves 2

2 veal escalopes
2 eggs
1 clove of garlic, grated
80-100g dried breadcrumbs (panko works well)
1 tbsp grated Parmesan
Salt and pepper
Groundnut oil, for shallow frying

Whisk the eggs and garlic together, then coat the veal in the egg mixture. If you have time, leave it there for 10 minutes.

Mix the breadcrumbs and Parmesan together, then season the veal generously. Coat the veal in the breadcrumb mixture, making sure it's completely covered.

In a very large frying pan, heat 3mm of oil. When hot and almost smoking, carefully place the veal into the oil and cook until golden on one side. Don't be tempted to turn it too early, and keep it still so it creates a golden crust.

Cook for roughly 3 minutes on each side and serve immediately.

Tips
Milanese can also be made with pork or chicken, butterflied and flattened until thin. The latter will need to be cooked for longer.

Don't overcrowd the pan. It's better to do it in batches. Use more oil than you think you need.

Mum's Christmas Eve Lamb Curry

In 1986, when Mum first made this Christmas Eve curry, finding the right spices and lamb neck fillets was no easy feat; every ingredient was sourced from specialty shops. It was a labour of love, saved for special occasions. Here, I've added a modern twist – Christmas Eve deserves a little flair.

Preparation time – 20 minutes
Cooking time – 2 hours
Serves 4-6

700g lamb neck fillets, cut into 5cm chunks
Salt and pepper
2 large red onions, chopped, plus 1 for garnish, sliced
6 cloves of garlic, crushed
1 thumb-sized piece of grated ginger
2-3 red chillies, finely chopped
6 cardamom pods, bruised
2 tsp ground coriander
2 tsp ground cumin
1 tsp chilli powder
1 tsp ground turmeric
1 tsp mustard seeds
4 medium tomatoes, finely chopped
300g chestnut mushrooms, quartered
1 block of coconut cream, sliced into small pieces
2 tbsp Greek yoghurt
400ml chicken stock
Pomegranate seeds, to serve
Fresh coriander, to serve

Preheat the oven to 160°C fan/180°C conventional.

Season the lamb with salt and pepper, and in a large casserole dish, start by browning the lamb in batches and then set aside.

Add the chopped onions to the pan and turn the heat to low. Sauté the onions until soft and caramelised. Introduce the garlic, ginger and chilli and cook for one minute. Add all of the spices to the pan, stir and cook for another minute.

Return the lamb to the pan along with any juices on the plate. Add the tomatoes and mushrooms and cook for 2 minutes. Throw in the creamed coconut, yoghurt and pour in 300ml of the stock. Stir to melt the coconut.

Bring to a simmer, place a lid on and cook in the oven for 2 hours or until tender. Stir halfway through the cooking time and top up with extra stock if necessary. The tomatoes and mushrooms should release enough liquid.

Finish with pomegranate, coriander and sliced red onion.

My Dad's New Zealand Mussels in the Half Shell

A memory I'll never forget involves a sack of mussels, a bathroom, and an old gastropub in Kent. Back in the '80s, I'd scrubbed the mussels in the bathtub (no sink was big enough!) for my dad's menu, inspired by our annual trips to the Balearics and a taste of rustic Mediterranean life. In those days, a menu with something like this was certainly different.

Preparation time – 5 minutes, plus defrosting time
Cooking time – 15-20 minutes
Serves 2 as a main meal, or 4 as a starter

16 precooked, frozen New Zealand green-lipped mussels
Salt and pepper

For the garlic butter

300g butter, at room temperature

4 cloves of garlic, crushed

2 tbsp finely chopped flat leaf parsley

2 tbsp grated Parmesan

3 tbsp panko breadcrumbs

Lemon wedges, to serve

Defrost the mussels in a colander slowly at room temperature. Then drain on kitchen towel to remove any excess moisture.

Preheat the oven to 210°C fan/230°C conventional.

Mix the garlic butter ingredients together in a bowl.

Lay the mussels in a large roasting tin flesh side up. Add a teaspoon of the garlic butter to each mussel and spread over the entire shell. Season well, particularly with black pepper. Cook in the hot oven for 15 to 20 minutes or until bubbling and golden brown.

Chicken Noodle Soup

This is the ultimate soul food. Mum's version was pure comfort – a bowl of warmth, goodness and nostalgia. That wonderful aroma drifting through the house felt like a hug in a bowl. It's what I grew up on, and my boys don't know life without it. If anyone's unwell, there's only one remedy.

Preparation time – 15 minutes
Cooking time – up to 2 hours
Serves 4

1kg chicken drumsticks, wings *or* a whole chicken, seasoned with salt and pepper
4 small onions, finely chopped
4 cloves of garlic, crushed
5 sticks celery, finely chopped
5-7 carrots, peeled and chopped
1 tbsp plain flour
2 litres water
Salt and pepper
250g dried noodles
200g peas
2 tbsp soy sauce
5 spring onions, sliced, to serve
(1.5 litres chicken stock if using leftovers)

Colour the seasoned chicken in a large casserole pan. This helps create great flavour. Remove and set aside.

Add the onion to the pan and gently soften. Add the garlic, celery and carrots to the pan and cook for 5 minutes. Season generously. Stir in the flour and return the chicken to the pan.

Cover with water (approximately 2 litres) and bring to a simmer, then cook without a lid for 1 hour for wings, 1 hour 30 minutes for drumsticks, or 1 hour 30 minutes to 2 hours for a whole chicken. Taste the stock and see if you think it needs reducing. If you don't think it has enough flavour you can add half a stock cube. Season to taste.

Take the chicken out of the pan and carefully remove the meat from the bones and return to the soup. Add the noodles, peas and soy sauce and cook for 5 minutes. Finish with the spring onions.

Tip
You can also use leftover cooked chicken for this soup. First sauté the onions, garlic, carrots and celery. Add the flour, followed by the chicken stock, and simmer for 30 minutes. Add the noodles and leftover cooked chicken for the last 3 to 5 minutes.

Mum's Quiche

My mum's quiche is the best, honestly it is. During the '80's I remember sampling dreadful quiches that were too eggy, with tough pastry bottoms. My mum's was nothing like this, instead filled with lots of goodies and full of amazing flavour.

Preparation time with pastry making – 30 minutes

Cooking time – 1 hour

Serves 4-6

For the shortcrust pastry

250g plain flour

140g cold cubed unsalted butter

1 egg yolk

2 tbsp ice cold water

Pinch of salt

Or

1 sheet of ready-rolled shortcrust pastry

For the filling

2 small onions, finely chopped

8 slices of streaky bacon, finely chopped

Salt and pepper, to taste

2 large eggs

2 egg yolks

275ml single cream *or* full-fat milk

1 tbsp finely chopped herbs such as dill, coriander, *or* chervil

100g Gruyère cheese *or* strong cheddar, grated

You will need

10 inch flan dish

For the shortcrust pastry

Sieve the flour into a large mixing bowl. Add the cold cubed butter and mix with your (cold) fingertips until you have a crumb consistency.

Mix together the water and egg yolk with the salt and gradually add to the pastry. You may not need all of the egg/water mixture. Bring together with your hands without over working. Form a ball and cover with cling film and chill in the fridge for at least 30 minutes to rest.

For the filling

Preheat the oven to 180°C fan/200°C conventional.

Carefully roll out the pastry to fit the flan dish, roughly 4mm thick. Press down to make sure the pastry is touching the flan dish. Prick the base and press the sides with a fork.

Bake in the oven for 20 minutes.

Sauté the onion until soft and sweet. Push the onion to one side and add the bacon and cook until golden. Season with salt and pepper.

Beat the eggs and mix with the cream. Season with salt and pepper and add the herbs.

Add the onions and bacon to the bottom of the pastry case and spread evenly. Sprinkle with cheese and then pour in the egg mixture.

Turn the heat down to 170°C fan/190°C conventional.

Bake in the oven for 35 to 40 minutes or until golden and set.

Remove from the oven and allow to cool slightly before serving.

Tip

When making the pastry, ensure that everything is cold. Cube the butter and then place in the freezer for 5 minutes before using. Make a double batch of the pastry and store in the freezer for 3 months.

The more colour on the onions the tastier the end result.

 Nostalgia Recipes

Ultimate Prawn Cocktail

A timeless starter, prawn cocktail brings a touch of retro charm to Christmas Day. With succulent prawns, a creamy, tangy dressing and a hint of freshness, it's a perfect opener for the holiday feast. My version is full of little goodies!

Preparation time – 15 minutes
Makes 4

300g cooked Atlantic prawns, without shell
4 large, cooked prawns, with shell
200g cooked tiger prawns, without shell
2 baby gem lettuces, torn
1 avocado, diced and coated with a squeeze of lemon juice
1 pot salmon roe
1 lemon, sliced into wedges

For the Marie Rose sauce

250g mayonnaise
1 tbsp ketchup
1 tsp Worcestershire sauce
$\frac{1}{4}$ tsp smoked paprika

Mix the Marie Rose sauce together and set aside, then pat all the prawns dry on some kitchen paper. Toss the Atlantic prawns with the sauce.

Layer the lettuce at the bottom of 4 glasses and top with avocado. Spoon over the prawn mixture. Top with the tiger prawns and salmon roe. Hook a large prawn over the side of each glass and add a slice of lemon to each to serve.

Tip

Serve in martini glasses or coupe glasses for extra sophistication.

Pork and Chutney Sausage Rolls

Nothing beats a homemade sausage roll, even with a little cheat like ready-rolled puff pastry. These savoury bites are perfect for Christmas party season – make extra batches, as they freeze well before baking. Ideal for soaking up sherry or fizz, because really, who doesn't love a sausage roll?

Preparation time – 10 minutes
Cooking time – 30 minutes
Makes 16-20

1 sheet of ready-rolled puff pastry
400g lean sausage meat
1 dessert spoon onion chutney
1 egg, beaten

Preheat the oven to 180°C fan/200°C conventional.

Unroll the pastry and cut in half lengthways. Split the sausage meat in two and spread it lengthways in the middle of each piece. Alongside each row of sausage meat, spread the chutney. Bring the long edges of the pastry together to encase the sausage meat between the pastry. Seal by pinching together with a fork all the way along. Using a sharp knife, cut each roll into 4cm sausage rolls. Then score each sausage roll at the top just through to the sausage meat.

Place on a lined baking sheet, brush with egg and cook in the oven for 25 to 30 minutes.

Tip
To get ahead, prepare the sausage rolls and freeze on a baking sheet. Once frozen transfer to a ziplock bag. Thoroughly defrost slowly in the fridge overnight and cook when needed.

French Dressing

In the late '80s, my dad and I joined a delightful French couple for lunch. Camille's salad – ripe tomatoes, goat's cheese, and an unforgettable dressing – was a revelation. She brought me into her kitchen to make a jar to take home, and I've made it that way ever since.

Preparation time – 5 minutes

Add everything to a jam jar and shake until it is all combined. If you have time, leave to infuse for 30 minutes at room temperature. If it separates, shake it again to bring it back together.

1 clove of garlic, crushed
1 heaped tsp Dijon mustard
3 tsp honey
1 tbsp white wine vinegar
4 tbsp extra virgin olive oil
Salt and pepper

Simple but Delicious Tomato Sauce

This is my go-to tomato sauce recipe – affordable and packed with flavour when you slowly caramelise the onions to a deep golden brown. I often make a big batch to use in different dishes. It lasts up to 5 days in the fridge and is a freezer essential! The world is your oyster with a sauce like this. I use it for the Fish Puttanesca on page 70 and the Aubergine Parmigiana on page 134.

Preparation time – 15 minutes
Cooking time – 50 minutes
Serves 2

2 small onions, finely chopped
Olive oil
4-5 cloves of garlic, crushed or finely chopped
1 tin of tomatoes
Salt and pepper

Sauté the onions in olive oil on a low heat with a little salt. Stir gently every so often, and cook until soft, sweet and caramelised.

If using an induction hob, you can really go slowly with this.

If using an Aga, cook on the outside of the lowest temperature hob.

Add the garlic and cook for 2 minutes. Pour in the tomatoes, season with salt and pepper and simmer with a lid on for 30 minutes.

If cooking on gas then you may need to add a little water as the sauce will dry out quicker.

Tip

If using a gas hob perhaps think about buying a heat diffuser.

Chicken Liver Pâté

My mum began making this pâté in the '70s for her and my dad's legendary dinner parties – the place to be, or so I hear! This recipe has stood the test of time, and she still makes it beautifully. Like those parties, this pâté is anything but subtle: rich, indulgent and full of flavour!

Preparation time – 10 minutes, plus 4 hours chilling
Cooking time – 30 minutes
Serves 4-6, as a starter

375g unsalted butter
3 banana shallots, finely chopped
400g chicken livers, trimmed
Salt and pepper
3 cloves of garlic, crushed
3 sprigs of thyme
1 tbsp brandy

Melt 50g of the butter in a pan. Add the shallots and cook until soft and sweet. Push the shallots to one side and add the chicken livers. Season with salt and pepper and cook until blushing.

Add the garlic, thyme and brandy and cook for 3 minutes.

Set aside 200g of the butter and some thyme leaves, then transfer everything else to a food processor and blend until smooth.

Spoon into little ramekins or jars.

Melt the remaining butter and pour over the pâté. Decorate with thyme leaves. Allow to cool completely before placing them into the fridge for about 4 hours before serving.

Serve with toast, chutney and cornichons.

Tuna Dip

Don't knock this one until you've tried it, because this dip is addictive. Imagine a bold, elevated tuna mayo. In our family, we love it with thick, quality crisps, or spread generously on toasted sourdough for an open sandwich, finished with a drizzle of extra virgin olive oil. Pure comfort.

Preparation time – 10 minutes

Serves 4, as a starter

1 tin of tuna in olive oil, drained

10 cherry tomatoes, finely chopped

1 small red onion *or* 6 spring onions, finely chopped

2 tbsp finely chopped dill

¾ tub of cream cheese

2 tbsp mayonnaise

Add the tuna to a medium bowl and mash using the back of a fork. Add the remaining ingredients and thoroughly combine.

Serve as part of a snacking board, on fresh bread, or as a topping.

Marie's Elderflower Loaf Cake

Our dear friend Marie passed away last year, and I think of her often, especially when I'm in the kitchen. We first met when my son Toby and her son Rory started nursery in 2006. I was a young mum, a bit out of my comfort zone, and Marie noticed immediately. She'd laugh remembering my petrified expression when we had to introduce ourselves at a PTA coffee morning, and she took me under her wing from that day on. Marie was the life and soul of every coffee morning, long lunch, and dinner party. She was an impeccable homemaker, following every recipe to the letter, which makes me truly sad she'll never read this book. Her cakes were the best – especially her elderflower cake, which she baked regularly for her coffee mornings. I never did get the recipe, but here is my version, in honour of a wonderful friend.

Preparation time – 15 minutes

Cooking time – 30 minutes

Makes 2 cakes (halve ingredients for 1)

For the cake

225g caster sugar

225g butter, at room temperature

4 eggs, at room temperature and beaten

3 tsp vanilla extract *or* vanilla paste

Zest of 1 lemon

225g self-raising flour

For the glaze

3 tbsp elderflower cordial

A squeeze of lemon juice

100g icing sugar

You will need

2 x 2lb loaf tins

2 loaf tin liners *or* parchment paper

Preheat the oven to 160°C fan/180°C conventional.

Cream together the caster sugar and butter until pale and light. Slowly add the eggs a drop at a time until fully incorporated. Add the vanilla and the lemon zest.

Fold in the flour, being careful not to lose any air gained. Split between the 2 lined tins and cook in the oven for 25 to 30 minutes.

Test with a skewer. If it's dry when you remove it, then the cake is cooked.

Mix together the elderflower cordial, lemon juice and icing sugar. Poke holes in the top of the cake with a skewer and pour the glaze over the sponge while it's still hot.

Leave to cool completely in the tin.

Auntie Sasa's Chocolate Pots

In our family, everyone brings something special to the table – quite literally! Auntie Sasa's dish was always her famous pudding. As kids, my cousins and I could hardly sit still through the main course, eagerly awaiting the moment she'd unveil the cherished highlight of every family gathering; her unforgettable chocolate pots!

Preparation time – 10 minutes, plus 2-3 hours chilling
Cooking time – 10 minutes
Makes 6

300ml double cream
200g dark chocolate, broken into pieces
2 egg yolks, whisked
2 tbsp brandy
20g unsalted butter

Warm the cream slowly and turn off the heat before it bubbles and boils. Add the chocolate and stir until completely melted. Allow to cool for 5 minutes, then pour in the egg yolks, brandy and butter and stir until smooth and glossy.

Pour the velvety mixture into ramekins or coffee cups and place in the fridge for 2 to 3 hours to set.

Cheat's Trifle

This nostalgic pudding is a Christmas staple, and I'm never sure if it excites the grown-ups or the kids more! It's less a recipe and more a fun assembly of shop-bought treats – super easy yet always a crowd-pleaser.

Preparation time – 10 minutes, plus setting time
Serves 6-8

1 packet raspberry *or* strawberry jelly
250g raspberries *or* strawberries
2 Swiss rolls, sliced into 3cm thick slices
2-3 tbsp sherry
2 -3 tbsp raspberry jam
500g custard
500ml double cream, whipped
Cherries, for garnish
Flaked almonds, for garnish

Make up the jelly according to the packet instructions. Pour into the bottom of the trifle bowl and add half the berries. Place in the fridge to set. When set, remove from the fridge.

Start by arranging the Swiss roll around the sides and then two layers at the bottom. Drizzle with the sherry and then spread with the jam. Now add a layer of raspberries, then spoon over the custard.

Lastly top with whipped cream and decorate with cherries and flaked almonds.

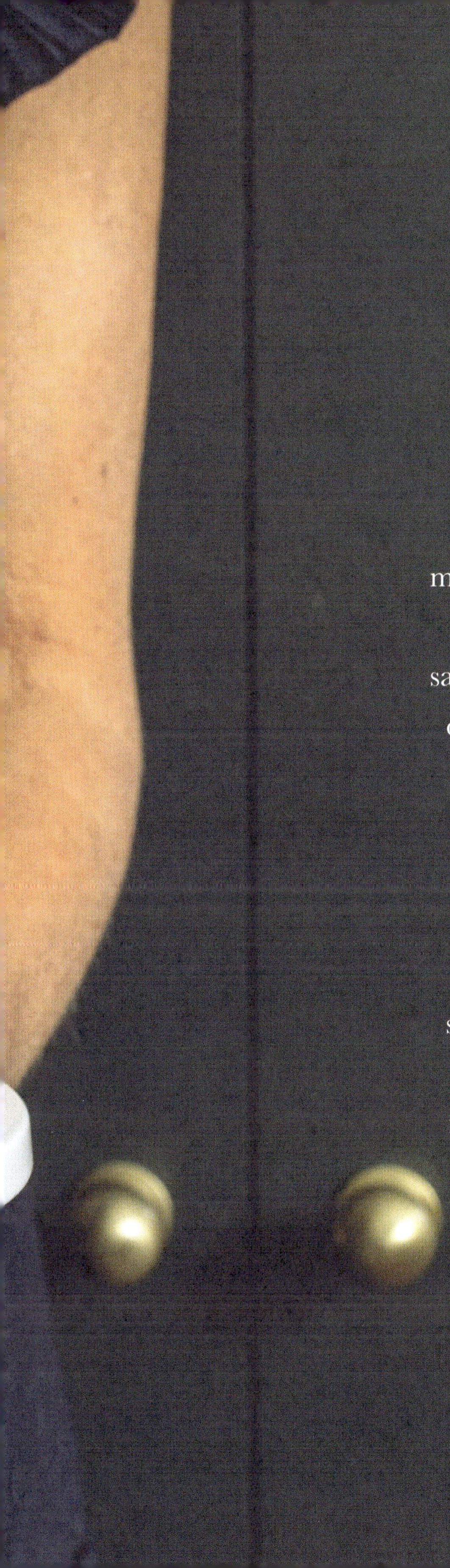

Desserts are the grand finale of any meal, and in my opinion, no cookbook is complete without a few show-stopping sweet treats. While I'm more of a savoury person at heart, I believe in enjoying a little of everything in moderation – including indulgent puddings. Whenever I pick up a new cookbook, I can't resist flipping straight to the dessert section, and I hope you'll feel the same way about this chapter. Now, I wouldn't call myself a baker – that's why the recipes here are approachable, straightforward, and designed to bring joy without stress. Whether you're looking for a simple midweek indulgence or a dessert to impress, you'll find it here, no science degree required.

Apple Tarte Tatin

This is one of my favourite desserts, best made with apples like Cox, Pink Lady, Braeburn or Jazz – avoid cooking apples for this one. Ready-rolled puff pastry keeps it simple and works wonderfully. Serve with crème fraîche or vanilla ice cream for a perfect finish.

Preparation time – 20 minutes
Cooking time – 1 hour
Serves 6

8 eating apples (I used Jazz apples)
75g unsalted butter
75g caster sugar
1 sheet of ready-rolled puff pastry

You will need

1 medium to large heavy-bottomed frying pan with metal handle

Preheat the oven 180°C fan/200°C conventional.

Peel, halve and core the apples.

Spread the butter on the base of the pan and sprinkle over the sugar. Add the apples curved side down, fitting them as snugly as possible as they are going to shrink.

Place the pan on the hob at a low-medium heat and wait for the sugar and butter to caramelise. Keep a close eye on the pan and aim for an amber colour – it's important that the caramel doesn't burn or turn bitter.

Once the caramel has formed, remove the pan from the heat and allow to cool slightly. Quickly cover the apples with the pastry, tucking in the edges. Be careful, the caramel is hot and there's no need to be neat.

Transfer to the oven and cook for approximately 25 to 30 minutes, or until the pastry is golden. Carefully remove from the oven and allow to cool for 15 minutes. Place a large plate on top of the pan and quickly flip. Hopefully it will come out in one piece!

Raspberry and Pistachio Eton Mess

This recipe brings a fresh twist to the classic, layering crunchy meringue, juicy raspberry and a luscious pistachio Chantilly. It's an easy yet elegant dessert, perfectly blending sweetness, creaminess and a hint of nutty richness.

Preparation time – 20 minutes
Serves 4

For the raspberry coulis

12-14 raspberries
Juice of ¼ a lemon
1-2 tbsp icing sugar

For the Chantilly cream

500ml double cream
1-2 tbsp icing sugar
1 tsp vanilla paste
1-2 tbsp pistachio cream

To serve

4 meringue nests, *or* see pavlova recipe on page 178 for homemade meringue
28-30 raspberries
2 tbsp pistachio nuts

Start by blitzing the raspberry coulis ingredients together, then pass through a sieve to remove the seeds.

Next loosely whip the cream, icing sugar and vanilla. Then ripple the pistachio cream through the Chantilly.

Roughly crush the meringue. Carefully mix the meringue, cream and two thirds of the raspberries in a bowl. Spoon into serving glasses or bowls.

Drizzle with a little coulis and finish with the remaining raspberries and pistachios.

"

Chocolate and Orange Banana Bread

Infused with the vibrant flavours of chocolate and orange, this banana bread offers
a delightful twist on the classic. The sweetness of ripe bananas blends with rich
dark chocolate and zesty citrus, making each slice a treat that's perfect for breakfast,
dessert, or any time in between.

Preparation time – 15 minutes
Cooking time – 50 minutes
Serves 4-8

140g butter, at room temperature
140g caster sugar
3 ripe bananas, mashed
2 eggs, beaten
140g self-raising flour
1 tsp baking powder
100g dark chocolate chips
1 tsp vanilla paste
Zest of 1 orange

Preheat the oven to 160°C fan/180°C conventional.

Cream the butter and sugar together until pale and light. Mash
the bananas and mix them in. Slowly pour in the eggs a drop at a
time until fully incorporated. Next fold in the flour, baking powder,
chocolate chips, vanilla and orange zest.

Pour into a lined loaf tin and bake in the oven for 45 to 50 minutes.

When the cake starts to fully crack at the top this is a sign it's cooked.
Check with a skewer, if it's dry when removed you are good to go.

Remove from the oven and allow to cool for 10 minutes in the tin
before cooling on a wire rack.

Strawberries and Cream Cake

This strawberry and cream cake layers light sponge with fresh strawberries, cream
cheese frosting, and a luscious spread of strawberry jam. It's a delightful dessert that
is my go-to celebration cake, and if you're part of my circle, you will have enjoyed
this many times.

Preparation time – 20 minutes
Cooking time – 30 minutes
Serves 6-8

For the sponge

227g caster sugar

227g soft butter, at room temperature

4 eggs, at room temperature

227g self-raising flour

2 tsp vanilla paste

For the frosting

200g full-fat cream cheese

100g soft butter

1 tsp vanilla paste

100g icing sugar

For the cake

Strawberry jam

Fresh strawberries

Preheat the oven to 160°C fan/180°C conventional.

Grease two sandwich cake tins, with removable bottoms.

Start by creaming the caster sugar and butter together in a mixer on
a high speed, until pale and light. Beat the eggs and add a little at
a time to avoid curdling. When the egg is fully combined, stop the
mixer. Now carefully fold in the flour and vanilla paste – try not to
knock out the incorporated air. Split the cake mixture between the
2 tins and bake for 25 to 30 minutes. Ensure the cake is fully cooked
by pricking with a cocktail stick – if it comes out clean, the cake is
cooked. Remove the cakes from the tins and allow to cool.

While the cakes are cooling, add the cream cheese, butter and vanilla
paste to a bowl and beat with a wooden spoon. Add the icing sugar in
small increments.

Spread jam on one half of the cake and frosting on the other, keeping
some frosting back for the top. Add a layer of sliced strawberries (keep
a few whole to decorate the top) and sandwich the two together.

Top with the rest of the frosting and decorate with halved
strawberries.

Carrot Cupcakes

These cupcakes are a warm, spiced treat, with cinnamon, ginger, and a sprinkle of pistachios. Moist and flavourful, they capture the essence of classic carrot cake in a perfectly portable form – a little indulgence for any occasion.

Preparation time – 20 minutes
Cooking time – 30 minutes
Serves 8-10

For the batter

230g self-raising flour

230g light brown muscovado sugar

70g pistachio nuts

1 tsp baking powder

1½ tsp ground cinnamon

½ tsp mixed spice

½ tsp ground ginger

260g carrots, grated

3 medium eggs, whisked

155ml light olive oil, plus extra for greasing

Zest of ½ an orange *or* lemon

For the icing

50g butter, softened

200g full-fat cream cheese

100g icing sugar

1 tsp vanilla paste

30g pistachio nuts, for decoration

Preheat the oven to 160°C fan/180°C conventional.

In a large bowl, mix the dry ingredients, and in another, mix the wet ingredients. Mix them together, combining thoroughly until smooth, with no lumps. Divide the mixture between 12 to 14 muffin cases in a muffin tin. Cook in the oven for 20 to 30 minutes. Remove from the oven and allow to cool completely.

Beat the butter, cream cheese, icing sugar and vanilla until velvety. Spoon over the frosting and finish with crushed pistachios.

Tip

This recipe gives you enough batter to make a full-size cake in two sandwich tins instead of the cupcakes if you prefer.

Pavlova with Chantilly Cream and Summer Fruits

With a crisp shell and soft centre, this pavlova topped with Chantilly cream and summer fruits is an ideal warm-weather dessert. Light cream and fresh berries balance the sweetness, creating a delightful mix of flavours and textures.

Preparation time – 30 minutes
Cooking time – 1 hour, plus cooling time
Serves 6

For the meringue

4 eggs
250g caster sugar
1 tsp white wine vinegar
1 tsp cornflour
1 tsp vanilla paste

For the cream

300ml double cream
1 tsp vanilla paste
1 tbsp icing sugar

To decorate

Strawberries, halved
Blackberries
Cherries

Preheat an oven to 150°C fan/170°C conventional.

Line a baking sheet with parchment paper. Draw a large circle on the paper. This will be the template for your meringue.

Separate the eggs, placing each white in a cup or small bowl before adding it to the whisking bowl. Discard the yolks or refrigerate them for another use.

Whisk the egg whites in a clean mixing bowl on a medium speed, until you have stiff peaks. Continue mixing on a medium speed, adding 1 tablespoon of the caster sugar at a time until fully incorporated. Add the vinegar, cornflour and vanilla and mix thoroughly. The meringue mix should be stiff and glossy by the time the sugar has been completely added, and you should be able to hold the bowl upside down without the meringue falling out.

Spoon the meringue mixture onto the parchment paper, making sure the perimeter is deeper than the centre.

Cook for 1 hour, then turn the oven off and leave the meringue to completely cool inside the oven. This helps the meringue to dry out. Don't be tempted to open the oven. Sometimes I leave it there overnight.

Whip the double cream, vanilla and icing sugar to form soft peaks, then spoon the cream into the centre of the meringue. Top with the strawberries, blackberries and cherries and enjoy.

Tips

Make sure the mixing bowl is completely clean and free from grease.

Damp and humidity can affect the meringue, so don't open the dishwasher while making the meringue.

If you can, make the meringue a day ahead and let it cool and dry out completely in a cold oven.

Lemon Possets

Bright, silky, and wonderfully simple, lemon possets are a timeless dessert that highlight the fresh, tangy flavour of lemon and creamy vanilla. With just a few ingredients, this velvety treat is both elegant and satisfying, a lovely finish to any meal.

Preparation time – 10 minutes
Cooking time – 5 minutes
Makes 6

600ml double cream
150g caster sugar
Juice of 2½ lemons
½ tsp vanilla paste *or* vanilla seeds
Zest of 1 lemon
2 tbsp caster sugar, to brûlée (optional)

Bring the cream to a very gentle simmer in a saucepan on the lowest heat. Add the sugar and dissolve, continuously stirring.

Turn off the heat, then add the lemon juice and the vanilla and stir to combine. The acid in the lemons will naturally thicken the cream. Strain the mixture through a sieve into a jug. Now pour into individual ramekins, glasses, coffee cups or lemon halves. Finish with lemon zest and leave to cool before placing in the fridge to set.

If adding a brûlée topping, sprinkle each posset with sugar and melt the sugar with a blowtorch until golden. Allow to cool and harden before serving.

Tip

These possets can easily be made the day before, removed from the fridge 20 minutes before serving, and then brûléed for a crisp crust.

Pistachio and Raspberry Cake

Pistachios are my weakness, from yoghurt toppings to pistachio cream. Here, they shine in a moist sponge paired with raspberries and cream cheese frosting. The result is a perfectly balanced, stunning dessert.

Preparation time – 20 minutes
Cooking time – 35 minutes
Serves 8-10

For the cake batter

170g butter
200g caster sugar
5 egg whites
1 tsp vanilla paste
175g ground pistachios
1½ tbsp Greek yoghurt
250ml full-fat milk
275 self-raising flour
1 tsp baking powder
1 tsp matcha powder (for colour)
½ tsp salt

For the frosting

50g butter, at room temperature
200g full-fat cream cheese, fridge cold
100g icing sugar
1 tsp vanilla paste

For the filling

1 tbsp raspberry jam
3 tbsp raspberries, to taste
1 tbsp pistachios, ground (for decoration)

You will need

2 x 21cm loose-bottomed cake tins

Preheat the oven to 160°C fan/180°C conventional.

Cream together the butter and sugar until pale and light. Add the egg whites and mix together for 2 minutes. Add the vanilla, pistachios, yoghurt, milk, flour, baking powder, matcha and salt and stir to fully combine.

Grease the tins and share the cake mixture between the 2 tins. Bake in the oven for 30 to 35 minutes or until cooked all the way through. Remove from the tins and allow to cool completely.

To make the frosting, beat together the ingredients until smooth.

Spread jam over the top of one of the cakes, followed by 1½ tablespoons of the frosting. Sandwich the cakes together, then top with the remaining frosting, and decorate with raspberries and pistachios.

Tip

To ensure a smooth lump-free frosting, make sure the butter is at room temperature and the cream cheese is straight from the fridge. Also don't be tempted to use low-fat cream cheese or the frosting will be runny.

Coconut, Mango and Cardamom Rice Pudding

This luscious rice pudding brings together the warm spice of cardamom, the delicate aroma of vanilla, and the vibrant sweetness of mango. Coconut milk replaces dairy for a rich, silky finish, creating a dessert that feels indulgent yet refreshing – a beautiful balance of exotic and comforting.

Preparation time – 5 minutes
Cooking time – 30 minutes
Serves 4

250g pudding rice *or* risotto rice
800ml coconut milk
1 tsp vanilla paste
$\frac{1}{4}$ tsp ground cardamom
$1\frac{1}{2}$ tbsp caster sugar, or to taste
150g-200g fresh mango, diced
Chopped mint, to garnish
1 lime, zest only

Combine the pudding rice, coconut milk, vanilla, cardamom and sugar in a medium-large saucepan. Bring to a gentle simmer, place the lid on and turn the heat to low. Simmer for 25 to 30 minutes or until the rice is cooked and creamy, stirring occasionally. If things look a little dry, then add extra coconut milk or water to loosen.

Mix the mango with the rice pudding and serve in individual glasses, finishing with a few mint leaves and lime zest.

Tip

Have a little extra coconut milk to hand just in case the liquid evaporates too fast. If you cook with gas, I'd really recommend using a diffuser to ensure things don't burn.

Plum, Cardamom and Vanilla Cake

The combination of vanilla and cardamom here works an absolute treat. It's the perfect cake to make from late summer all the way to Christmas when stone fruits are in season. I think of this as more of a grown-up cake, but having said that, I've seen many children devour a slice or two.

Preparation time – 20 minutes
Cooking time – 30 minutes
Serves 8-10

For the sponge

227g caster sugar

227g soft butter, at room temperature

4 eggs, at room temperature

2 tsp vanilla paste

1 tsp ground cardamom

227g self-raising flour

2 plums, finely chopped

For the filling and topping

600ml double cream

1-2 tbsp icing sugar

1 tsp vanilla paste

1 tsp ground cardamom

3-4 plums, finely sliced

Preheat the oven to 160°C fan/180°C conventional.

Grease 2 sandwich cake tins, with removable bottoms. Alternatively, line the tins with parchment paper.

Start by creaming the caster sugar and butter together in a mixer on a high speed, until pale and light. Mix the eggs and add a little at a time to avoid curdling. Spoon in the vanilla and cardamom. When the egg is fully combined, stop the mixer. Now carefully fold in the flour – try not to knock out the incorporated air. Split the cake mixture between the 2 tins, add the chopped plums and bake for 30 minutes. Ensure the cake is fully cooked by sticking a cocktail stick in the middle, and if it comes out clean, the cake is cooked. Remove the cakes from the tins and allow to cool completely.

Whip the cream until light and fluffy, adding the icing sugar, cardamom and vanilla halfway through. Be careful not to over whip.

Add cream to one half of the cake, then add a layer of sliced plums. Top with more cream and finish with more sliced plums.

Chocolate Chip Cookies

I wanted these cookies to be loved by both kids and adults, so I crafted a recipe that's classic, crunchy, crisp, and not overly sweet. Inspired by a version my mum made back in 1989, with help from my kids as taste testers, I'm proud to share this.

Preparation time – 15 minutes
Cooking time – 15 minutes
Makes 12-14

100g butter, at room temperature
110g caster sugar
1 egg, beaten
1 tsp vanilla paste
100g plain flour
$\frac{1}{2}$ tsp bicarbonate of soda
$\frac{1}{2}$ tsp salt
100g dark chocolate chips *or* chocolate chunks (don't choose anything with a high percentage of cocoa)

Preheat the oven to 160°C fan/180°C conventional.

Cream the butter and sugar together until pale and light. Slowly incorporate the egg and vanilla a bit at a time until fully combined.

Sift the flour, bicarbonate of soda and salt into the mixture. Fold together until fully incorporated. Lastly, fold in the chocolate chips.

Line 2 baking sheets with parchment paper.

Scoop heaped teaspoons of the cookie dough onto the baking sheets, leaving plenty of space around each one. Place 5 to 6 scoops on each sheet. They will spread out a lot and end up being approximately 10cm in diameter.

Cook in the oven for 10 to 15 minutes or until golden. Remove from the oven and carefully remove with a spatula and leave to cool on a wire rack. They will crisp up as they cool.